LEADVILLE:
A Miner's Epic

Stephen M. Voynick

MOUNTAIN PRESS PUBLISHING COMPANY
Missoula 1984

Copyright © 1984
Stephen M. Voynick
Revised 1988

Third Printing, September 1992

Library of Congress Cataloging in Publication Data

Voynick, Stephen M.
    Leadville: A Miner's Epic

    Bibliograpy: p.
    Includes Index.
    1. Leadville (Colo.) — History. 2. Mines and mineral
resources — Colorado — Leadville — History.   I. Title.
F784.L4V69 1984   978. 8'46   84-2001
ISBN 0-87842-171-8 (pbk.)

Mountain Press Publishing Company
P.O. Box 2399 • Missoula, MT 59806
Toll Free 1-800-234-5308

This book is for my father.

Other books by Stephen M. Voynick

The Making of a Hardrock Miner Howell-North

In Search of Gold Paladin Press

The Middle Atlantic Treasure Coast The Middle Atlantic Press

FOREWORD

I first visited the city of Leadville, Colorado, in the winter of 1970. I worked as a hardrock miner and lived at the old Vendome Hotel on Leadville's historic Harrison Avenue. Looking back, I found that year was a memorable experience, in fact, it was an education. I learned many things from the city and its people, but the most important lessons I learned were on the 600 Level of the Climax Molybdenum Company mine. There, within the rock confines of Bartlett Mountain, I learned to drill, to blast, to muck, and to timber. And in return for my shifts in the underground, I earned the wages of a Climax miner.

Like many before me, I recognized that Leadville was a very unusual city, a place where superlatives like the highest, the richest, and the oldest seemed commonplace. Although the vibrancy of a modern mining industry surrounded me, I found the city itself deeply rooted to the memories and monuments of an extraordinary mining past. Leadville took her birth from the gold mines, her fame and fortune from the silver mines, and she takes her continuing survival today from modern hardrock mines that produce molybdenum, silver, gold, lead, and zinc.

Living in Leadville, I could touch every day the reminders of that great history. Fascinated by the visible history, I turned to the libraries in search of more. I readily found glowing accounts of the legendary H. A. W. Tabor, of the visit of President Benjamin Harrison, and stories of the likes of Jesse James and Doc Holliday, and of the lonely, heartbreaking vigil of Baby Doe. Page after page echoed the sound of gunshots in boisterous saloons, of soprano voices ringing through a packed Tabor Opera House, of the clatter of hoofbeats announcing the arrival of a Denver stage, and of the long, mournful wail of a narrow gauge locomotive whistle from a snowy mountain pass. The books were filled with visions of ivory dice flashing across green velvet, of Victorian architecture rivaling the grand buildings of the East, and of endless stacks of silver bars waiting for shipment.

The Leadville story is a first rate frontier epic, with romance and excitement enough for ten cities, but a vital element was missing. In all those pages and books, the silver bars seemed to appear as if by magic, for the historians had stopped at the mine portals. The story they missed is the real story of Leadville: the story of the mines and the men who worked them, of thundering rock drills and dynamite fumes, of how metals were torn from mountains in a grim, determined, and too often tragic effort that ranks among the greatest of all frontier achievements. And though there are few stage lights and little tinsel, it is not a common story, for these were not common men. Common men could not have met the task of driving hundreds of miles of underground workings through hard rock at elevations of more than two miles above sea level. These were exceptional men, men with qualities as tough and enduring as the rock they conquered. Yet the historians, limited by an ignorance of the underground, have given them only a secondary position in history, when truly it is the everyday working miner who was, and who still is, the heart and essence of Leadville.

Mining has never been romantic or fun, and anyone who implies it is has never mined. It is dark, dirty, demanding, and dangerous. This book will take the reader beyond the portals and down the shafts for a glimpse of a different world, the world of the hardrock miner. Along the way, it will recount the Leadville epic from a different perspective, one devoid of the traditional glamor and romance.

Since Leadville's story is basically a tale of men tearing metals from mountains, the story must begin with the mountains themselves.

> *Stephen M. Voynick*
> *Leadville, Colorado*
> *August, 1983*

CONTENTS

FOREWORD v

THE HIGHEST VALLEY OF THE ARKANSAS...................1

PART I: THE GOLD MINERS.................................5

PART II: THE SILVER MINERS.............................27

PART III: THE MOLYBDENUM MINERS 87

PART IV: THE PRESENT 123

SOURCE ESSAY...155

GLOSSARY...158

INDEX...161

I hold it a noble task to rescue from oblivion those who deserve to be eternally remembered.

— Pliny

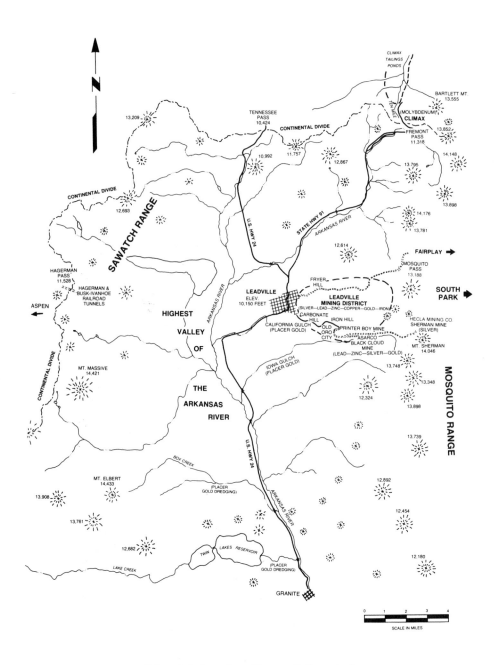

The highest valley of the Arkansas

THE HIGHEST VALLEY OF THE ARKANSAS

Sixty-seven million years ago the crust of the earth in the western United States buckled in a massive upheaval. Great blocks of granite were thrust upward to form the Rocky Mountains, the final step in an even lengthier period of geological formation. The region where Leadville, Colorado, would someday stand was lifted upward on one of the most dramatic movements on the entire continent, eventually achieving stability more than two miles above the level of the distant, receding seas.

During these formative ages, great pressures forced upward hot, mineral-bearing liquids into crustal cracks where cooler temperatures and lower pressures caused solidification. As these minerals crystallized out of solution, they accumulated along cracks and fracture surfaces in mineralized veins. Continuing crustal movements folded, crushed, and faulted the rock, creating channels where water and solutions could leach, alter, concentrate, and eventually redeposit many minerals into complex bodies. Among the many minerals to reach the surface in this manner, three have a particular relevance to our story – gold, silver, and molybdenum.

In central Colorado, the Rockies were formed as a series of ranges running north and south. In the east, the granite walls of the Front and Sangre de Cristo Ranges abruptly ended the rolling expanse of prairie. To the west rose the Park Range. Between these primary ranges were three broad basins: North, Middle, and South parks. Even further west stood the most awesome uplift in the entire system, the Sawatch Range. And nestled in the heart of these towering granite peaks lay a

1

beautiful and secluded mountain valley.

Life, although still primitive, adapted quickly to the slopes and waters of the Rockies. Once the mountains were geologically stable, water assumed the major role in sculpting them to their present form. The mountains trapped the moisture of the westerly winds, bringing it to earth in summer as rain and in winter as the snow that would forever cloak the highest peaks. Drop by drop, the waters came together, first as tiny rivulets, then as small streams that began to wear away the rock that caused their birth. And in a high alpine meadow, in the shadow of a peak whose crumbling granite slopes hid a core of white rock streaked with black, a tiny bubbling stream of crystal water began its long journey.

Twelve thousand feet above sea level, the clear icy waters of the Arkansas River first flowed together in a small, rushing torrent only a few feet wide. There were no trees in this alpine world, and the waters splashed through a low, tundra-like growth that the brief summer turned to a carpet of brilliant color woven from a million wildflowers. During the long winter the tiny stream rested, locked lifelessly in ice beneath a mantle of snow. Still a small stream, the Arkansas raced down through lower, dense forests of pine and spruce, past groves of white-trunked aspen, steadily widening as it entered a high mountain valley. In its first twelve miles, this dashing mountain stream had descended 2,000 feet, and with time it carried away great quantities of silt and gravel to build the valley floor.

Worn away with the rock was a yellow metal contained within. As fine dust, tiny flakes, and even some sizeable nuggets, the heavy yellow bits were tumbled over and over in the stream gravels, always working their way closer to bedrock. There, hidden beneath the common gravels, the concentrated, gleaming yellow layers waited patiently for the time when their discovery would alter both the lives of the river and the men who would walk its banks. The restless waters worked also on a white metal, physically and chemically transforming it within the rock into veins and massive bodies of a heavy, black carbonate mineral.

In that first and highest mountain valley of the Arkansas River, the stream slowed its pace and grew broader as other streams contributed their waters. Now ten feet wide, the crystal water sparkled in the sun and skipped effortlessly over the rocky bed. At times the stream paused in deep, secret pools, but only to race again across green meadows of the valley floor. The valley was ten miles long and three miles wide, bordered on the west by the 14,000-foot Sawatch Range and on the east by the 13,000-foot peaks of the Mosquito Range. The valley floor itself was 10,000 feet above sea level, with an alpine climate that brought snow from November to May, but also a summer that was a joyous explosion of color and life. Wildflowers bloomed in profusion as deer, elk, buffalo, bear, beaver, and bighorn sheep roamed the valley. Grouse, ptarmigan, turkey, and waterfowl nested, and fish thrived in the clear waters of the Arkansas.

No longer a mere stream, the Arkansas River quickened its pace to slash a canyon through solid rock. In a rage of white foam, the river left its highest valley with a chorus that thundered off the naked rock walls. Seventy miles from its alpine source, the river turned east to carve a grand monument to its own power – the Royal Gorge, a sheer, 1,000-foot deep gash in solid granite to fittingly mark the end of its tenure as a mountain river. Beyond the Gorge, the Arkansas grew quiet, and waters that once danced over mountain meadows now crept sluggishly across the vast prairies toward the Mississippi, and finally to the sea.

Long after the river was ancient, man first walked its banks. Only the mysterious, dark-skinned Utes, the nomadic hunters of the high mountains, followed the Arkansas to its source. The highest valley was valued religiously by the Utes. Arriving in June, they harvested game, skins, fish, and berries through the summer, departing for lower valleys only when the chill winds of October announced the onset of winter. In their ideal co-existence with nature, a symbiosis the land would never enjoy again, they treated the valley and the river well, and in return were provided with their simple necessities of life. As an utterly practical people, the Utes had no need for the bits of yellow metal in the stream gravels. And even after centuries of use, the mountains remained unscarred and the water continued to flow clear and pure.

Known only to the Utes, the highest valley of the Arkansas River was a hidden place of great beauty, guarded by granite mountains, carpeted with rich grasses and wildflowers, forested with pine, spruce, and aspen, and watered by a free mountain river. Unnoticed by the Indians, as it had been since the creation of the mountains, the water continued to wear down the rock and deposit the bits of yellow metal in the stream gravels. The river had done its job well, and now those bits of gold were ready for the coming of the white man.

PART I

The Gold Miners

Clad in shapeless but comfortable mocassins and tattered skins, and cradling a long-barreled Kentucky rifle, the lone figure struggled slowly upward over the jumble of barren granite. Breathing heavily in the thin mountain air, James Purcell paused to rest, lowering himself slowly onto the lichen-covered rocks.

Pleasantly aware of the sun's warmth, Purcell faced east, his eyes sweeping over the great green basin of South Park. Four years had passed since he had left his native Bardstown, Kentucky, bound for a vague land called simply "the West." With the clothes on his back, a rifle, and a small parcel of personal belongings, he had set out for the Mississippi. Along the bustling St. Louis waterfront he had first heard the bold tales of the West, of enormous herds of game, of rushing rivers, and of beaver so profuse that trappers could make their fortunes in only two winters. But most intriguing had been the tales of the "shining mountains," peaks so tall that even in summer they gleamed with snow.

5

The first to see those great mountains had been the Spanish; failing in their search for gold, they had still laid claim to the entire region and established a trading post at Santa Fe. Next had come the French, claiming all the land from the Mississippi west to the unexplored "Great Divide." The French relinquished their claims in 1763, but independent French adventurers had already reached the eastern base of the Rockies by every major stream from Mexico to Canada. Although concerned primarily with furs and Indian trade, the French had also detected the presence of gold. In 1758, Le Page de Pratz, in his *Histoire de la Louisiana*, made clear mention of a *Min d' or*, or gold mine, on the upper Arkansas River, telling of a "rivulet whose waters rolled down gold dust," although it remained uncertain whether the origin of his report was Indian legend or an actual journey by a Frenchman to the highest valley of the Arkansas River.

Purcell shifted the familiar weight of the Kentucky rifle in his arms. With his legs rested and his breathing again regular, it was time to be moving. He lingered another moment, his thoughts still back in St. Louis where he had joined a hunting party bound for Kansas. There, Indians stole their horses. Purcell and his group launched a foolish but successful attack on a Kansa village, recovering most of the horses and earning the name "crazy Americans." He then joined a party of French trappers moving up the Missouri River toward the Mandan country. But for Purcell, the lure of the shining mountains was greater than that of trapping profits, and he began a year-long journey up the South Platte River. From a site near the present city of Denver, James Purcell first viewed the shining mountains.

During those years of lonely adventuring, his appearance and manner had become more Indian than white; only his beard, lighter skin, and omnipresent Kentucky rifle distinguished him from the plains Indians he accompanied. Driven from the plains by marauding Sioux, he had lived for two years in South Park with a small band of Kiowas. He had explored every corner of South Park and, near the site of the future town of Fairplay, had dug into the gravels and discovered placer gold. Purcell had been more amused than excited for, in the world in which he now lived, gold was rather worthless. True value was found in game, warm skins, and his dwindling supply of black powder and lead balls. Still, he collected the tiny bits of yellow metal, placing them in his shot pouch and expecting maybe someday to return to civilization.

Purcell resumed climbing, drawing strength now from the anticipation, for no Indian could tell him what lay beyond this granite range. Finally, on a summer afternoon in the year 1803, James Purcell stood atop the 13,000-foot Mosquito Range, mesmerized by the panorama before him. Far below to the west was a deep valley of incomparable beauty through which flowed a mountain river reflecting the sun like a living silver ribbon. Beyond the valley rose the most massive range of mountains he had yet seen. Purcell knew instinctively that this was the Great Divide, beyond which the waters would flow west to the Pacific.

Purcell studied the valley, imagining the abundance of game and wondering if those streams might contain gold, too, and vowed to be the first to explore it. As it was, James Purcell had already accomplished many firsts; he was the first American to reach the Rocky Mountains by crossing the Great Plains, the first to discover gold in the Rockies, and the first to view the highest valley of the Arkansas River. But his exploration of that valley would have to wait, for the sun was already sinking toward the peaks of the Great Divide. James Purcell turned back east, descending the granite slopes of the Mosquito Range toward South Park.

Purcell never did explore that highest valley, for he was soon captured by hostile Indians. After escaping, he wandered far to the south where a group of Apaches finally led him to Santa Fe. Although displeased and concerned by the presence of an American, the Spanish authorities allowed Purcell to remain. He spent the remaining nineteen years of his life as a carpenter at the Spanish post.

And what of the gold that he carried for months in his shot pouch? In a dark moment when he had grave doubts about survival, much less of ever returning to civilization, James Purcell threw it away.

The next Americans to penetrate the central Rockies were members of a United States Army exploration party commanded by twenty-seven-year-old Captain Zebulon Pike. Leaving St. Louis in July, 1806, Pike followed the Arkansas into the Rockies and by December — nearing the worst of the high country winter — reached the confluence of Lake Creek. From a hilltop, Pike saw the river's highest valley, but prudently yielded to the weather and turned back south. Pike's official government report of 1810 offered a rare glimpse of the still pristine upper valleys of the Arkansas River in words that reveal a sensitivity for the land as well as an ecological awareness far ahead of his time.

. . . from the entrance of the Arkansas, in the mountains, to its source, a distance of about 170 miles; (by the meanders) it is alternately bounded by perpendicular precipices and small narrow prairies, on which the buffalo and elk have found the means to survive, and are almost secure from danger from their destroyer — Man.

The borders of the Arkansas River may be termed the paradise (terrestrial) of our territories, for the wandering savages. Of all the countries ever visited by the footsteps of man, there was never one probably that produced game in greater abundance . . . and I believe that there are buffalo, elk, and deer, sufficient on the banks of the Arkansas alone, if used without waste, to feed all the savages in the United States territory one century.

Several months later, Spanish soldiers escorted Pike to Santa Fe where he chanced to meet James Purcell, whom he refers to as "Pursely." The mention of Purcell's gold discovery in Pike's reports aroused little public interest in the East; the nation was not yet geared economically, territorially, or emotionally to pursue stories of gold in the distant, mysterious West.

After 1810, a growing number of American adventurers and "mountain men" explored the Rockies. Most of their travels have gone unrecorded, but it is probable that a few wandering fur trappers reached the highest valley of the Arkansas. The first documented visit did not occur until 1845 when Colonel John C. Fremont, leading his third United States Army exploration and mapping expedition, followed the Arkansas past the point where Pike halted thirty-nine years earlier. In his memoirs, published in 1887, Fremont also made special note of the beauty and abundance of game in the highest valley.

. . . crossing various forks of the River we finally, on September 2d, reached and continued up the main branch, having on our right the naked rock ridge of the mountain, and encamped at night on the headwaters of the Arkansas in Mexican territory. . . .

This was pleasant traveling. The weather was now delightful and the country beautiful. Fresh and Green, aspen groves and pine woods and clear rushing water, cool streams sparkling over rocky beds.

In a pine grove at the head of the River we came to our delightful surprise upon a small band of buffalo, which were enjoying themselves in the shade and fresh grass and water. . . .

Time had about run out on the ages of peaceful seclusion for the highest valley of the Arkansas; even at the time of Fremont's visit, the nation was leaning toward the West, and the valley's inevitable date with history was drawing near. The most momentous event affecting the American westward movement was the discovery of

8

gold in California in 1848. The thousands of Americans languishing in the economically and socially depressed East suddenly had a viable alternative — go West. They did, by the hundreds of thousands, in ships, in wagons, and on foot, beginning the American love affair with gold on a grand note. The California gold production went beyond even the wildest hopes and, in only seven years, surpassed all that which the Spanish had taken from Mexico and South America in three centuries.

By 1851, rapid development had made California a State of the Union, but other areas of the West remained unpopulated and unexplored. Some of the original "Forty-niners," lured by the recurring reports of gold in the Rockies, dropped out of the California rush to prospect the Colorado foothills, but without success. By 1858, the California rush had run its course, leaving thousands wandering idly about the exhausted gold fields. Meanwhile, in the East, the financial panic of 1857, a prolonged drought that curtailed agriculture, and the uncertainties and fears generated by an impending Civil War again created rampant unemployment and gloom. The troubled United States needed, wanted, and was ready for another major western gold strike.

The strike was made in spring, 1858, on Cherry Creek near the future site of Denver. When word reached the East, the press, promoters, and guidebook printers worked overtime to publicize exaggerated reports of the fortunes in gold that waited in the streams of the new "El Dorado." By fall, the nation was primed for its second major gold rush, this one bearing the name of Pikes Peak, the dominant landmark of the new gold fields. In the spring of 1859, 100,000 wild-eyed "Fifty-niners," packing shovels, gold pans, and guidebooks, hit the trails for Colorado. Most found not gold, but disappointment that turned first to disgust, then to bitterness, as many wagons turned back over the prairies, their drivers cursing the name of Colorado and Pikes Peak. But the more determined gold seekers abandoned their disappointing claims on Cherry Creek and turned toward the Rockies. Hundreds of small bands of prospectors, following a flurry of rumors as well as their own intuitions, ventured west into the rugged canyons. Within weeks, many discoveries had been made that dwarfed the original Cherry Creek strike. The streams of the Rockies proved rich with gold; by fall, the mountains were dotted with a string of booming gold camps that included Idaho Springs, Silver Plume, Georgetown, Central City, Fairplay, Black

This early Colorado prospector-miner is representative of Leadville's first miners. Note the worn military overcoat, Sharps rifle, and worldly belongings packed on a rugged little burro. Colorado Historical Society

Hawk, and Breckenridge. At its worst moment, the Pikes Peak rush had been redeemed, and now Colorado Territory, like California a decade earlier, would enjoy accelerated settlement and development.

Through 1859, the highest valley of the Arkansas remained untouched by the army of gold seekers that rampaged through the lower, more accessible mountain regions, damming and diverting streams, cutting timber, and plowing roads in their fanatical quest for placer gold. But 1859 was to be the last year the game would abound, the timber would stand tall, and the Utes would visit their ancestral hunting ground on the banks of the Arkansas River. Although there is some doubt, most historians claim the first prospector to cross the Mosquito Range was a certain A. G. Kelley, to whom is attributed the discovery of placer gold in the Arkansas near the site of Granite. Neither the name, nor the act, was of any true significance, for whether or not he discovered gold in 1859, many prospectors would certainly have done so the next spring. It is not known if Kelley returned in spring, 1860, but five prospectors, S. S. Slater, George Stevens, Issac Rafferty, John Currier, and Abe Lee, broke their winter camp in March, moved across South Park, and crossed the snowy Mosquito Range to reach the Arkansas at Granite. Prospecting their way north, they moved into the highest valley where they discovered a bit of color at Colorado Gulch. Just a short distance further, they passed another stream with a trickle of open water flowing down from the foothills of the Mosquito Range.

At this point, there are several versions of the tale. The following is typical, and was recorded by a person with little practical mining experience, but with a pronounced romantic flair for the pen.

> When Abe Lee wearily sat up in his buffalo robe bedroll, the sun was already up, its bright, warm rays already melting the snowshelf overhanging the clear mountain stream that coursed through the gulch. Lee sleepily blinked his eyes and watched the drops of melting ice plop into the water. And he opened his eyes wide and scrambled for his gold pan. Winking up at him from the still pool of water set apart from the main stream by a beaver dam was a telltale glitter. As he poured away the water, bits of gold flakes covered the bottom of the pan.

This particular account is a good version of what did *not* happen, but one made popular because the press had learned that a bit of exaggeration and oversimplification sold more newspapers.

On the 8th day of April in 1860, when the five prospectors reached the gulch that would become known as California, the "warm sun" was not melting much ice. In early April, at 10,000 feet, dawn tem-

11

peratures are near zero; the weather is dominated by daily snow showers and occasional blizzards. Water temperature of the creeks, if they are running free at all, is near freezing. The water is numbing to the touch and the continuous immersion encountered in gold panning often results in a painful, arthritic-like tightening that even makes simple finger movement difficult upon wakening in the bitter cold mornings.

Just as there was no warm sun greeting Abe Lee at dawn, neither was there any gold winking at him from the gravels. Never confuse "panning" and "prospecting"; amateurs today "pan" for gold, but in Abe Lee's day, men "prospected." Before Abe and his prospectors ever bothered to pan for color, they dug into the gravels, and they dug deep. The romance of "panning for gold" diminishes rapidly when you consider the job that faced Abe Lee. More often than not, his laborious digging through many feet of frozen gravel produced nothing but pan after pan of worthless black sands with just enough tiny specks of color to hold his interest.

Abe and his partners worked their way up the gulch about one mile above the Arkansas. Digging again, they found a bit of color. Digging deeper still, they found a bit more. Finally after penetrating the frozen gravels nearly to bedrock, they struck pay dirt. When the last of the black sands from the deepest gravels were washed away, a small, but brilliant, yellow "foxtail" glittered from the edge of the pan. The discovery was in no way similar to the popular misconception of a gold strike; there was no wild screaming and backslapping as the prospectors danced jubilantly around a pan heaped with gold nuggets. Abe Lee's first "good" pans held about one gram — less than 1/30th of an ounce — and were worth about fifty cents, for raw placer gold was then worth about sixteen dollars per Troy ounce. Their discovery was merely promising, and it would be a month before the spring runoff would provide enough water to permit thorough evaluation of the gravels. At the time, not one of those five men had any real idea of just what they had discovered.

The first discovery claim was staked on April 12th; a mining district was formed, officers elected, and simple by-laws enacted. Within days, other prospectors straggled over the Mosquito Range to dig, pan, and stake. With ground sluicing and diversion techniques aided by increasing volumes of water, the prospectors soon worked their way to bedrock to discover gold that exceeded even their optimistic expectations. Some returned to South Park to notify friends

12

and secure supplies for a summer of mining at California Gulch, so named because it had "all the promise of California." From South Park, word of the strike spread down every stream and trail where men working mediocre gravels abandoned their claims, packed their gear, and headed for the highest valley of the Arkansas River. By May, 1,000 men swarmed around California Gulch where District Recorder Abe Lee recorded each new claim, using the funds received to erect the first cabin in the gold camp they named Oro City.

First in Denver, then weeks later in the East, the California Gulch strike was reported in the usual manner: men were taking gold with nothing but "pans and their bare hands." As for Abe Lee and his partners, the only report that ever rang of truth regarding their discovery appeared in the Leadville *Weekly Herald* twenty years later. It told of how gold had been struck in California Gulch in April, 1860, after prospectors had dug *twelve feet* into the gravels. And that is a pretty deep hole for "pans and bare hands."

When Abe Lee arrived, the banks of the seven-mile-long Gulch were lined with a coarse grass and the hillsides were densely forested with pine and spruce. By June, 4,000 men had marched into that pleasant mountain haven to stake 400 separate mineral claims, each 100 feet long, and every one an active placer mining operation.

Placer mining is nothing more than an adaptation of the basic process that deposited the gold in the first place. Its most intriguing and alluring aspect is the utter simplicity of technique and required equipment. The primary tool is the sluice box, a wooden trough about two feet high and wide and at least ten feet long, with its bottom lined with a series of laterally fixed ridges, or riffles. The sluice is positioned in the stream bed with the water flowing through it. Gold-bearing gravel is then fed into the front of the sluice; the heaviest materials plummet to the bottom to be trapped by the riffles, while the lighter common gravels are washed through. The sluice is really an artificial stream bed in miniature, for the principle of gold separation and concentration are the same in both. Efficiency of gold recovery is dependent upon proper water velocity; too great a velocity will cause loss of fine gold in the tailings; too little will clog the riffles with worthless common gravels.

To clean the sluice, the water is diverted away and the trapped material, or concentrate, is removed by hand. The concentrate is composed mainly of heavy minerals such as black iron sands, metallic lead, compounds of other heavy metals, and, hopefully, particles of

This photo, taken in 1860, tells a familiar story that was taking place in most Colorado creek beds. Placer mining was a lot of back-breaking pick and shovel work to move enormous quantities of gravel to recover the gold that lay hidden near bedrock.   Colorado Historical Society gold. Careful hand panning will further refine the sluice concentrate. The final step, the actual recovery of the gold, may be accomplished by further panning, magnetic removal of the black sands, or by mercury amalgamation which assures the recovery of even the finest gold dust. The end result, if there was gold in the gravels to begin with, is a varying quantity of the yellow metal ranging in size and shape from flour to flakes to grains to nuggets. What had taken the river eons to accomplish, the placer miner has managed in days. All the tools and techniques employed in the early years at California Gulch were already centuries old.

Although placer mining is simple, it is not easy. Almost always, the gold will be buried beneath a substantial overburden of worthless gravel, as Abe Lee could well testify. That stream bed overburden was composed of everything from the finest silt to gigantic boulders. Some could be moved by clever use of water, but most waited for two other ancient tools, the pick and shovel.

The narrow confines of California Gulch made disposal of waste rock, tailings, and boulders a problem, but it was the availability of water that became critical. Even during the runoff, the miners were woefully short of water because of the collective consumption of 400 active placer operations. Sluices on the highest claims released their discolored water to be used and re-used by every succeeding claim until it eventually reached the last claims at the base of the gulch as a trickle of mud. Along each claim, water was the subject of heated arguments. If one miner, for example, simultaneously operated three sluices on his claim, the lower adjacent claim received not one, but three reduced sources of water arriving at different points. Accordingly, a maze of trenches, flumes, and wooden aqueducts crisscrossed the gulch as mines sought maximum utilization of the limited water supply. Consolidated operation of adjoining claims eventually achieved greater efficiency, but in 1860 it was every man for himself, and there was little love among the miners of California Gulch.

The environmental effect of placer mining was disastrous, not that it was a consideration at the time. Trees by the thousands fell before the swinging axes, their trunks quickly whipsawed into rough planks destined for sluices, flumes, shoring to contain tailing heaps, and the primitive cabins springing up along the gulch. The banks of the gulch, where grass and trees had grown a few months earlier, became as barren as a lunar landscape. Aside from miners and mules, nothing lived among the undulating, endless piles of rock and gravel.

15

Since nearly every stream in the highest valley of the Arkansas showed color in the pan, none were spared. Streams that had flowed anonymously for ages were unceremoniously honored with names, then torn apart. The names given in 1860 still remain today: Iowa, Colorado, Evans, Birdseye, California, and many more. And each of those newly named streams now contributed silt and mud to the Arkansas.

Even though the entire gulch had been staked since spring, gold seekers continued arriving through the summer. The miners worked feverishly from morning until evening, driven by an awareness of the early onset of the alpine winter. Up and down the once quiet gulch, the collective mining activity created a cacophony of ringing axes, grating whipsaws, pounding hammers, and scraping shovels, and behind it all shouting, cursing, and a chorus of untrained, but enthusiastic rough voices singing the ballads of the day. Punctuating the din were sporadic loud reports from big bore Sharps rifles, aimed at passing deer who contributed venison for the miners' dinner plates.

Oro City had grown from a single cabin to a functional settlement in mere weeks. The term "city" was only an optimistic hope for the future, for the ugly cabins and mired streets had none of the opulence associated with latter day Leadville. The log cabins were chinked with mud; roofs were just high enough to clear a man's head and constructed of split logs covered with thick layers of grass and sod. Although the interiors were all dark, damp, and drafty, Oro City's cabins were still a warmer shelter than a wagon or tent. A few elaborate cabins sported oilcloth windows and simple porches to bridge the mud that waited outside the single door. Anthony D. Webster recorded his dismal impression of Oro City in his diary:

> Wednesday, July 18th, 1860 . . . Was surprised at seeing so large a town, where only a few weeks ago not a house was seen, and not a wagon ever made its track. Now the crooked street on both sides is walled up with log Palaces and at least 8,000 inhabitants claim this as their Mountain home until fortune favors them and their Purses become fat with the "filthy Lucre," the "Root of all Evil." Such is the rush for these mines when a new Gulch is discovered. . . .
> The streets appear as though everyone built his cabin in its own place without regard to survey and as a consequence they are very crooked. The mining portion of the Gulch is about six miles long and nearly every claim is being worked and at the store the sound of gravel and shovel is heard as they "wash out" with their "Toms." Have heard much about the population and rapid growth of these "fast cities" but to appreciate them one must see for themselves.

16

From the appearance should think that gamblers ruled the place, from the numerous "Hells" which they have erected. And from the general inhabitants of young "Oro" should judge they would hardly rank among first society.

Webster was referring to the same elements responsible for Denver's already notorious reputation — gamblers, prostitutes, purveyors of cheap Taos Lightning, and a good number of parasitic transients with no intention to work. Still, the rudiments of a local economy were established, based first upon the prodigious timber requirements of the miners. With rough lumber selling at the inflated price of twenty-five cents per foot, a man with a whipsaw could earn as much as, if not more than, his counterpart digging in the gravels. As in every gold rush, the fortunate ones were the early arrivals able to stake their own claims; the rest became laborers on another's claim for a daily wage of gold dust and, with luck, a bonus at season's end. Gold dust was the accepted medium of exchange in the few stores that sold basic commodities at outrageous prices.

Oro City may have found little approval among its few refined observers, but it did fulfill its basic purpose of providing a community for the miners. Many miners also fulfilled their basic purpose for, by September, $1,000,000 in gold had been washed from the gravels. With the value of refined gold fixed at $20.67 per Troy ounce, and the miners receiving somewhat less because of the impurities in their raw gold, that sum translates to 55,000 ounces, or 4,600 pounds. The total volume of gravels displaced in California Gulch and adjacent streams during that first summer exceeded 250,000 cubic yards, or tons. Yet the total volume of gold recovered, if it were melted down and cast, would be a single cube measuring eighteen inches on a side — a comparison useful in appreciating the enormous amount of work performed by the miners. No matter how the California Gulch production was expressed, it was a lot of gold, more than any other camp in Colorado. A good claim that first summer produced about $60,000, a veritable fortune in a time when $1,000 would buy a house on a choice piece of land in the distant East.

While the long summer of backbreaking work and coarse living conditions had miners cursing even the mountain bluebirds, their most illustrious oaths were reserved for the heavy black sands that quickly clogged their sluice riffles. Heavy boulders of what seemed to be the same mineral were common in the gulch; both the sand and the boulders were discarded with the tailings. While most miners only cursed their presence, a few questioned their composition, but with

17

the sciences of geology and mineralogy still rudimentary, the troublesome heavy mineral remained a mystery. Guesses ranged from complex iron compounds to a form of lead, and a few even suggested silver. No one really cared, for in the summer of 1860, men dug for gold.

Among those men was twenty-nine-year-old Horace Tabor. Twilight had descended over California Gulch to silence the day-long din of shovels, hammers, and saws. Tabor had paid his six laborers their daily wage of one dollar in gold dust, and now watched them march off down the gulch, probably to spend it all on Taos Lightning. He sat alone on the edge of a sluice box, swatting occasionally at the determined July mosquitoes. His back ached and his hands and feet were cold and wet. His claim, a confused pattern of trenches and rock piles, was not rich in comparison with some of the lower claims, but it had been one of the few sections open when he arrived on May 8th, 1860, and he was lucky to stake it.

For Horace Austin Warner Tabor, California Gulch was the end of a long trail that began in his native Vermont; it had led to a stint as a Maine stonecutter, then to an unsuccessful three-year effort as a Kansas farmer. When word of the Colorado gold strikes reached Tabor, his crops were never planted in the spring of 1859. Instead, he set off with his wife, Augusta, and their sixteen-month-old son, lurching across the Kansas prairies in an ox-drawn wagon bound for the new El Dorado. Tabor had first tried his luck in Idaho Springs and Central City and found little gold. Augusta cooked, baked, and sold milk from their four cows to tide the family through the winter of 1859. When Tabor returned to Idaho Springs in February, 1860, he found his claims jumped.

That misfortune proved a blessing in disguise; Horace Tabor returned to Denver, gathered his family, and set out again, this time to chase rumors of gold in the highest valley of the Arkansas River. The wagon trip into the mountains, across South Park, and over the Mosquito Range had taken two long, hard months. When they arrived at Oro City, the Tabors slaughtered their exhausted oxen to provide meat for the hungry camp. The miners had gratefully reciprocated, not so much for the meat, but in deference to Augusta, the only respectable woman in camp, and built the family a small cabin. While Horace worked his claim in the upper gulch, Augusta weighed gold, handled mail, cooked and served meals, washed laundry, and

18

took in boarders. Although hardly making a fortune, the Tabors were doing far better than the average gold seeker who rushed to California Gulch in 1860.

With a weary sigh, Horace Tabor turned to the daily job of cleaning the sluice box concentrates. Four buckets held nearly 100 pounds of heavy black sands washed from nearly ten tons of California Gulch gravel. Emptying one bucket into a gold pan, Tabor kneeled by the cold water and with a practiced hand worked the heap of black sand down until only a cup or two remained. After standing to stretch his back, wipe his brow, and swat the mosquitoes, he finished the other buckets. Consolidating all the concentrate into a single pan, he again bent to the water, panning until only two cups of black sand remained. In the last light of evening, he peered intently into the battered pan and gave it a graceful sweeping motion. The swirling water spread the black sand evenly around the pan, revealing first a faint glint of gold, then the awaited gleaming yellow foxtail. The sight of the gold elicited no smile, just a silent, somber estimation of quantity. The gold recovered by seven men performing ten hours of backbreaking work filled three, perhaps four, teaspoons — about four ounces, close to his average daily take. His laborers had taken six dollars, expenses another two. Horace Tabor, stonecutter and farmer now turned placer miner, had netted another fifty dollars.

By the end of September, 1860, Tabor had washed out over 300 ounces of placer gold worth about $5,000. It was not a bonanza, just a respectable reward for the summer's work. But the highest valley of the Arkansas held far more for H. A. W. Tabor; it would be his name alone, of all the 10,000 gold seekers drawn to California Gulch, that would live in the history books.

When the approach of winter forced the miners to the lower camps, they left behind a valley that had changed more in six months than nature could have managed in centuries. California Gulch had been literally turned over in the frantic search for gold; all the adjacent streams had been dammed and diverted, and now the rocky bottom of the Arkansas lay covered in a bed of silt. Forests had been turned to fields of ugly, foot-high stumps. The herds of deer had been decimated to fill the stomachs of 10,000 white men and the buffalo were gone forever from the area. No Ute Indian fearful of his life would ever again venture into his sacred ancestral hunting grounds in the highest valley of the Arkansas.

19

The Pikes Peak rush brought the formal creation of Colorado Territory in 1861. At the first meeting of the Territorial Legislature, Lake County was established as an enormous tract of land from the Mosquito Range to the distant Utah border that included one-third of the entire Colorado Western Slope. The settlement at Granite, not the far larger Oro City, was made the county seat. Oro City seemed to have everything against it; it was shut off from the outside world for half the year and the only access was over treacherous mountain passes. Considering collectively the transportation difficulties, the physical problems associated with the extreme elevation, the six months of frozen isolation, and its shady reputation, few believed that the highest valley of the Arkansas would ever host a stable and respectable city.

Beginning with the spring runoff, 1861 was a repeat performance of the preceding year; when the last of the sluice concentrates had been washed, another $1,000,000 in gold had been recovered. By this time, the main road to Oro City from Fairplay had been built over the Mosquito Range, a twisting, hair-raising wagon trail topping out at 13,188-foot Mosquito Pass, the highest mountain pass in North America. True to the expectations of the "flatlanders" in the lower camps, Oro City remained purely functional. It existed solely to serve the placer miners during the six months of annual mining activity, and boasted none of the refinements that were appearing in other camps. Oro City's cultural and recreational outlets remained drinking, gambling, whoring, and fighting, and all were pursued vigorously until winter snows triggered the annual exodus. The million dollar production of 1861 would never be achieved again. No one knew it, but Oro City, before it was ever really born, was already dying.

During 1861, several gold lode deposits were discovered in upper California Gulch. They appeared as outcrops of white quartz containing visible gold. Miners crudely exploited the outcrops, attacking the quartz with picks, crushing it with hammers, then recovering the gold either by washing or amalgamation. At least one unsuccessful attempt was made to tunnel into the side of a hill in pursuit of a quartz vein. Although several lode claims were staked, the time was not yet ripe to begin mining hardrock deposits.

The year 1862 was the last good year at Oro City, producing just under $1,000,000 in gold. The next year, gold recoveries declined dramatically and it was generally agreed the gravels were nearly exhausted. In 1865, the cumulative production of placer gold since the strike had reached $4,000,000, but current production was negligible. Oro City, dreary in its good years, was now absolutely dismal. Only a small part of the annual throng returned to rework the old gravels or, hopefully, to locate small pockets of overlooked pay dirt. All that remained of Colorado's richest placer camp was a long string of deserted and decaying cabins and the scattered refuse of the boom days: old boots, broken shovels, rotting canvas, discarded bottles, and piles of slowly bleaching boards that had once been sluices and flumes.

By 1865, a transition was underway in the highest valley of the Arkansas, in Colorado, and throughout the mining West. Previously, the term mining meant placer operation, but now that many gravels had been exhausted, miners became interested in lode deposits. Even as Oro City languished in 1865, the West's first great adventure in underground, or hardrock, mining was already underway at Virginia City, Nevada, where the huge Comstock silver deposits had been discovered. Reports of silver in Colorado were becoming more frequent and, by the late 1860s, it was known that the troublesome heavy mineral that had clogged the sluices in California Gulch was some form of silver. Assayers, however, could not determine the correct composition, nor could metallurgists suggest suitable smelting methods. If Colorado mining were to regain its economic importance, it was clear that major technological advances would be necessary.

The mining transition became apparent in two immediate ways. First, the age of the enterprising individual as the backbone of western mining was drawing to an end. No longer would a man equipped only with a pick, shovel, and gold pan, together with a bit of luck and determination, stand much chance of becoming a producing miner. Some rich gravels would still be discovered, but the glory years of placer mining were history. Secondly, the future of mining was shaping up as a cooperative industrial effort involving engineers, metallurgists, heavy equipment, mills and smelters, a new breed of miner, and a reliable transportation system. Transportation would be vital if the Rockies were to achieve their mining potential. The lumbering wagons and stages that crept precariously over the high mountain passes would be totally inadequate for the coming years. Success in mining Colorado's lode deposits would be largely dependent upon the coming of the railroad.

21

A portent of the future appeared in upper California Gulch in 1868 when two experienced miners, Charles Mullen and Cooper Smith, turned again to the lode deposits that had been staked seven years before. Using the crudest of tools, they drove slowly into the hard rock, following rich, but elusive, gold-bearing veins. When they began producing outstanding specimens of white quartz shot through with delicate wires of yellow gold, a flurry of lode prospecting began. Quite suddenly, several hardrock mines — at least the forerunners of today's hardrock mines — were operating near Oro City. All were humble efforts by later standards, severely limited by an ancient technology and the mountain transportation problems. Short horizontal tunnels, called *drifts*, and shallow vertical workings, called *shafts*, tried valiantly to follow the mysterious wanderings, the frustrating disappearances, and the encouraging reappearances of the gold-bearing veins. Rarely, if ever, was the width of a drift wider than the spread of a man's arms, and for good reason. Smaller drifts provided better ground support and required less timber to stabilize the workings. The final consideration was the sheer effort needed to "break rock."

Since the hard rock would yield to no pick, the early hardrock miners drilled and blasted. In 1868, "drilling" was a misleading term; it was the same ancient procedure used by the Missouri lead miners for decades, the tin miners of England before that, and even by the Spanish gold miners in the 1600s. Drill holes were made manually; a miner simply held a chisel-like steel in one hand while swinging a four-pound sledge with the other. This "single jacking" technique could be speeded by "double jacking," where one miner held the steel and one or even two of his partners rhythmically swung eight-pound sledges. After each hammer blow, the miner holding the steel would "shake," or rotate it a fraction of a turn to reposition the cutting edge. Holes were never drilled much deeper than two feet, since the time required for a single hole could be one hour, although it varied greatly with the hardness of the rock and the enthusiasm of the drillers. And since the average "face," or working end of a small drift, required at least seven holes, hand steel drilling took most of the miner's time and effort.

After drilling, the miner loaded the holes with black powder, an ancient mixture of saltpeter (potassium nitrate), sulfur, and charcoal with a few minor "modern" additives to improve performance. Unlike modern dynamites, black powder is a deflagrating explosive, mean-

22

ing the explosive effect is created by rapid burning within a confined space. In use, the black powder was packed in paper cartridges and gently tamped in place, always with a wooden stick to assure there would be no potentially disastrous sparks. With the fuse extending outward, the miner then packed each hole with mud. The timing of each charge was of great importance, for if all exploded simultaneously, the energy would be "shotgunned" uselessly down the drift. A logical sequence was employed. The center holes, closely grouped and angled together to meet within the rock, were exploded first to blast out a center "burn." The remaining outer charges could then also direct their energy inward, breaking the rock in keeping with the desired configuration of the drift. Timing was achieved by the miner lighting each fuse in sequence, or by first cutting each fuse to the appropriate length and lighting all simultaneously.

Before blasting, the miner laid a flat iron sheet in front of the face to provide a smooth working surface for later removal of broken rock, or muck. With all in readiness, the miner lit the fuses, shouted the traditional "Fire in the hole!" warning, and quickly retreated to safety. If all went as planned, the drift would be advanced about two feet and four tons of muck awaited the shovels (and backs) of the miners.

This system of breaking rock would have been simple enough, if it were not performed in the underground. In the early lode mines of California Gulch, light was provided by candles mounted in sconces, or spike holders, jammed into crevices and timbers. The light was barely enough to see by, a worrisome matter for the miner holding the steel as his partner savagely swung the sledge at a very small target — the one-inch-diameter steel only inches away from his hands and wrists. The lack of ventilation presented another problem. Two exerting miners and several candles quickly depleted the oxygen in the narrow confines of the underground, a condition which worsened with every foot the drift advanced from the portal. Each blast also generated a thick cloud of noxious fumes, carbon monoxide, smoke, and dust, all of which lingered for hours in the stagnant air and was routinely inhaled by the miners. The systems of intersecting shafts and drifts later used for a cross circulation type of ventilation were, in 1868, considered non-productive and an unaffordable expenditure of time and effort. The western hardrock era was just beginning, and already the future lot of the hardrock miner looked none too pleasant.

A small group of hardrock gold mines, most backed by the first eastern capital to reach Oro City, was operating near upper California Gulch in 1869. The first was the Printer Boy, soon joined by the American Flag, the Five-Twenty, and the Pilot Tunnel. The cabins of Oro City obligingly migrated up the gulch to be nearer to the mines that seemed to promise the town's salvation. A small stamping mill was erected to crush the ore, the first ore treatment facility in the highest valley of the Arkansas. The upper gulch now echoed with the sounds of the neophytic hardrock industry; from within the mines came the ring of hand steels, and from outside the hiss of boilers, the gasping clatter of steam engines, and the heavy, rhythmical pounding of the stamping mill. Some ores contained gold in particles large enough to be recovered after crushing by simple sluicing. The ores with finer gold present had to be shipped by wagon over Mosquito Pass to the better milling and recovery facilities of the larger camps. As the mines went deeper, ores became more highly refractory with less free gold. Mine owners could ship only the highest grade ores to the experimental smelters near Denver. In 1869, Oro City's hardrock mines were an unfortunate step ahead of both mining technology and mountain transportation.

The Printer Boy and the American Flag returned profits, but nothing on the scale of the placer fortunes eight years earlier. As the mines grew, so did the problems of development. Aside from the ventilation difficulties (which the Printer Boy may have eased somewhat by venting raw steam into the underground to circulate air), another problem appeared that would plague hardrock mining forever. As the mines went deeper, the accumulation of water increased tremendously. Unable to cope with the water, miners watched helplessly as lower workings flooded, then resigned themselves to working the higher deposits only.

The year 1870 found Oro City with only some twenty families, most scraping a living from the troubled hardrock mines or the few placer operations. Officially, the camp boasted "fifty miners, and several saloons, eating houses, and corrals." Among those who returned in the renewed hope of 1868 were the Tabors. When the California Gulch gravels began playing out in 1862, the family moved back over the Mosquito Range and reestablished their store in Fairplay. But when the opening of the Printer Boy and its sister mines had many believing Oro City would boom again, H. A. W., Augusta, and their son, already nine years old, returned. Unfortunately, Oro City did not boom, and its bleak prospects were reflected in the opinion that a

24

prominent Denver merchant held of Tabor himself: "He is an honest man and will pay his bills when he can; but what business can he do in Lake County? There isn't enough business there to keep a cat alive."

Oro City may have been stagnant, but the nation was not. A terrible Civil War had been fought to its bloody conclusion and a reunited country embarked upon its final westward surge. The Indians who had proven so troublesome in their innocent and heroic efforts to hold their historic lands, had been mostly contained or eliminated entirely, although a few tragic, decisive battles remained to be fought. The distant east and west coasts had been first tied together by a group of courageous pony riders carrying the United States Mail, then by a thin copper telegraph wire. Finally, in 1868, a golden spike was driven to mark the completion of the transcontinental railroad. Even as the persistent ring of drill steel echoed from the portal of the Printer Boy in forgotten Oro City, a similar ring sounded across the Colorado prairies as spikes were driven to hold the rails that would bring the first iron horse to Denver. And as the discarded, well-cursed heaps of the heavy, black "waste" rock lay in California Gulch oxidizing slowly in the successive alpine seasons, chemists and metallurgists in the East and in Europe pried steadily at its secrets.

Not even the most ebullient optimist in Oro City, of which there were very few in 1870, could imagine what the next few years would bring. If ever the stage of history had been set extravagantly for the next act, it was so set in the highest valley of the Arkansas River. It was unfortunate that so little documentation of Oro City existed, for that tough little settlement was about to become engulfed in both name and being by a maelstrom of humanity, chaotic excitement, and wealth that would never again be matched in the history of the West.

PART II

The Silver Miners

In the early 1870s, the mining fortunes of Oro City paralleled those of the Territory in general. Declining gold production had dimmed the once golden image of Colorado. Disillusionment and caution were common among mining men and among the eastern financiers who would have to provide the needed capital if hardrock mining were to grow. The silver era began without the chaotic excitement of the Pikes Peak rush, opening slowly and in pace with technical advances in amalgamation and smelting processes that made possible steadily increasing silver production. Only when it was shown that silver could indeed be profitable did the conservative grip holding eastern capital loosen. Silver was known in most Colorado gold districts, occurring in deposits of varying richness and composition. The honor of becoming Colorado's first booming silver camp went to the remote alpine town of Caribou, fifty miles northwest of Denver. Caribou's fame was brief, for its production was quickly eclipsed in 1874 when rich silver ore was struck at Georgetown. Frenzied development

27

brought Georgetown new mines, mills, smelters, and even the arrival of the railroad in 1877. That year, Georgetown stood alone as the undisputed Silver Queen of the new State of Colorado with an annual production of $2,000,000.

Interest in western hardrock mining intensified with South Dakota's Black Hills gold rush in 1876 which soon produced millions from both placer and hardrock mines. Further encouragement came from a series of Colorado silver strikes at Alma, in Park County, and in the southwest where smelters were under construction at Ouray, Silverton, and Lake City. Excitement grew as miners intuitively believed a bonanza strike was imminent, and that their camp would displace Georgetown as the leading silver producer. No one could foretell the magnitude of the silver strike that would soon be made at old Oro City; if they had, they would have closed their portals, shut down their furnaces, and rushed for the highest valley of the Arkansas River.

Even as late as 1875, not even Oro City itself knew what was coming, and its few remaining miners worked at gold. Two partners, William Stevens and Alvinus Wood, believed California Gulch was still rich enough to warrant further mining, but only on a volume basis. Stevens, a promoter, had first visited Oro City in 1865, but found little to hold him. Wood, an accomplished technical mining man, arrived in Oro City in 1874. That year, they formed a partnership that was to prove very effective; Stevens provided the capital, Wood the technical expertise. The two partners began a "hydraulicking" operation in California Gulch, using large pumps and high pressure water jets to erode away stream and alluvial banks and pass huge quantities of gravel through large sluices.

To solve the water supply problem, they constructed a $50,000, eleven-mile-long aqueduct to divert water from the Arkansas headwaters to California Gulch. The arrival of the water brought the sounds of placer mining to the gulch once again, but this time the scrape of the shovels could hardly be heard above the throb of the pumps and the roar of the water jets. The operation profited for a number of years, and the sluice riffles still clogged rapidly with that "damned" black sand which by now was recognized as a lead carbonate bearing "some silver."

While their crews worked the sluices, Stevens and Wood prospected, taking samples from outcrops in the upper gulch that seemed to be the source of heavy black sands. Assays revealed a content of

28

40% lead and as much as 20 to 40 ounces of silver per ton. In 1875, lead was worth 6¢ per pound and silver $1.16 per Troy ounce, making the outcrops worthy of further investigation. In any more accessible camp, this ore would have been mined immediately, but the highest valley of the Arkansas still lacked roads and smelters. So at considerable expense, small loads of high grade ore were hauled by wagon to the railhead at Colorado Springs for shipment by train to smelters in St. Louis. Encouraged by the results, Stevens and Wood quietly acquired other lode claims. Late that year, a small smelter to treat simple ores was erected at the base of the gulch near the Arkansas. It was the area's first smelter, and was built near a group of cabins already achieving an identity separate from Oro City.

In 1876, new arrivals began sinking shallow shafts, often encountering respectable lead-silver values in the local carbonate deposits. Spring snows were still deep in 1877 when assayers began reporting lead values of 50% and silver sometimes reaching 100 ounces per ton. Growing interest attracted more miners and the cabins near the base of the gulch began to look like a *bona fide* town. Seeing visions of greatness for the little camp, a more suitable name than Slabtown was in order. Leadville was chosen in belief that the mining future rested with lead.

In summer of 1877, prospectors moved north from the gulch toward three low hills soon to bear the names of Fryer, Iron, and Carbonate. The prospectors (really prospector-miners, for at this stage in mining, a man had to be both) sank exploratory shafts, little more than glorified holes with dimensions of three by five feet, just enough to permit single or double jacking. The miners drilled directly into the rock floor of the shafts, or downholed, using water and small spoons to clear the holes of drill cuttings. As the shafts deepened beyond the point where the miner could conveniently shovel the muck out, he erected a simple log tripod overhead and fitted it with a sheave wheel. He then passed a hemp rope over the sheave wheel and tied it to a metal bucket. The toplander, the miner handling the surface chores, could then haul the bucket to the surface, as long as the load did not exceed his own weight. Improvement came with the windlass which provided a degree of mechanical advantage enabling the toplander to lift heavier loads. The windlasses were first powered manually, but as shafts deepened and loads increased, horses and mules were put into service. The miner fitted the shaft with a timber collar at the surface to stabilize the surrounding ground and provide safe footing

The era of hardrock mining began with the simplest of equipment. This simple log "A" frame was the forerunner of the heavier and more elaborate headframes that are a common site in Leadville today. Note the horse-powered whim and the sheave wheel at the top of the "A" frame. In mines of this type, the shaft dimensions were barely large enough to allow passage of the ore bucket which carried ore, waste rock, equipment, and men.

Colorado Historical Society

for his toplander. If the rock below required support, the miner installed crossbraced logs for the depth of the shaft.

The miner sank his exploratory shaft "blind," that is, without any assurance that paying ore, or "mineral" would be found. If the miner had reason to expect the presence of a laterally located mineral body, he drove narrow drifts off from the shaft. Shaft sinking was difficult and slow, but in 1877 in Leadville the miner did not have far to go, for he was sitting atop one of the world's richest and most accessible lead-silver deposits. One of those early shafts would strike high grade mineral at just sixteen feet. Assay reports became incredible; lead values of 50% were accompanied by hundreds of ounces of silver per ton. When several more strikes were made, the word was relayed over the mountains to every mining camp. The word was silver, in quantities and richness never seen before.

A larger horse-powered whim serving the declined tunnel of a Leadville mine in the 1880s.   Colorado Historical Society

The winter of 1877-78 was spent gearing up for the coming monumental hardrock mining adventure. By spring, the population of Leadville had doubled, then tripled as more newcomers arrived daily. In Denver and the East, financiers put their capital on the line, gambling that the glowing reports coming out of the Colorado Rockies, from someplace called Leadville, were true. Columns of freight wagons began winding their way over the high passes to Leadville bearing the tools of the new mining era, products of the past decade of technological advance made when the highest valley of the Arkansas River had been all but forgotten.

Explosives were the first innovation to affect hardrock mining. In 1846, an Italian chemist discovered nitroglycerin, a clear, oily liquid with more available energy pound for pound than any other material then known to man. But nitroglycerin was as unstable as it was powerful; thermal change or the slightest physical shock could trigger instant decomposition and the release of enough energy to destroy everything in the immediate vicinity. The first attempts to find industrial, military, or technical applications for nitroglycerin were abandoned. In 1860, the Swedish chemists Immanuel and Alfred Nobel also experimented unsuccessfully with nitroglycerin, but in the course of their work invented the first reasonably safe blasting cap. Their first caps were made of tin, then of copper, and employed fulminate of mercury, a compound hardly more stable than nitroglycerin itself.

In 1866, George Mowbray built the first nitroglycerin manufacturing facility in the United States in Pennsylvania. The same year, Alfred Nobel achieved a breakthrough in his experiments to tame nitroglycerin by mixing the liquid with porous, absorbent diatomaceous earth. The resulting solid explosive was not nearly as shock sensitive as straight nitroglycerin, yet could be detonated by Nobel's fulminate of mercury blasting caps. The new explosive was called "dynamite," and although a great advance in explosives, it was still an extremely hazardous material.

Since one-quarter of the early dynamites was composed of inert filler, the explosive strength was considerably reduced. Other fillers were found that contributed to the available energy of the explosive; in 1875, Nobel dissolved colloidal cotton in nitroglycerin to produce a gelatinous mass with two major improvements; it was much more powerful, and it was the most stable form of nitroglycerin yet devised.

Dynamite and the newer gelatin dynamites were all "high," or detonating, explosives: that is, they required a high explosive shock, such as that from a blasting cap, in order to detonate. The impulse of dynamite explosions was much sharper, creating a shattering effect to break rock into smaller, more easily handled pieces than the large, cumbersome ones produced by the slow, heaving effect of black powder. Most importantly, the new dynamites were five times as powerful as black powder, and fully worthy of the name "giant powder" by which they became universally known.

Dynamites were manufactured in convenient paper cartridges to fit drill holes and, by 1875, were already in use in many hardrock mines even though they retained serious drawbacks. Compared with modern explosives (which we still refer to as "dynamite"), the early compounds were so shock sensitive that railroads positively would not haul giant powder for ten years after its introduction. Transportation of "giant" was limited solely to the lurching, jolting freight wagons where the mule skinner more than earned his pay. The noxious cloud of gases and fumes that accompanied detonations was another problem, and soon began to fell miners working underground. Even without detonation, miners working with giant frequently suffered splitting "powder" headaches. This phenomenon would, in later years, be attributed to the manner in which nitroglycerin relaxed capillaries and caused an increased flow of blood to the brain, hence, a severe headache. But the most glaring fault of all, as time would soon tell, was a terrible thermal instability caused by the high freezing point of nitroglycerin.

By 1878, when Leadville was booming, mining had about completed its transition from black to giant powder. And the already proven reliable Bickford black powder fuse, the fulminate of mercury blasting caps, and the now familiar red sticks of giant powder were the tools of the blaster's trade.

Giant powder could break rock as nothing before, but still could not be used to its full potential because holes drilled by the slow hand steel techniques were only about two feet in length. Yet all that would soon change, for the greatest single advancement ever made in hardrock mining was at hand.

Steam power had first been used in mining in Cornwall, England, and, since the late 1700s, had powered a variety of mechanical devices. When the first experimental rock drills appeared, it was steam that powered them. Among the earliest was a crude machine built by Issac Singer in 1838. Singer's drill was a steam piston arrangement lifting a heavy drill rod, then allowing a free gravity fall, a system which sufficed only for vertical drilling. Singer could not perfect his rock drill, but went on to achieve eventual success in a more delicate area of mechanics — sewing machines. Then, in 1846, J. Couch patented a steam drill with an automatic valve permitting power on both the forward and backward strokes, thus suiting it for horizontal drilling also. Couch's drill was impractical because of its great weight —- over a ton — and high cost. By 1851, European drills had been designed to operate on either steam or compressed air.

The direct forerunner of the modern rock drill was built by Charles Burleigh, John W. Brooks, and Stephen F. Gates, and was patented in the United States in 1866. Adaptable to either steam or compressed air operation, the drill was fairly compact and employed a single piston traveling back and forth within a cylinder. An automatic trip valve reversed the entry of steam (or air) at the end of each stroke, thus propelling the piston-drill steel unit in the opposite direction. This was the "hammering" action of the drill; the rotary action necessary to reposition the cutting edge of the steel was accomplished manually with a miner turning a wrench as the drill pounded away. First employed on rail tunnel projects in the East, the drill proved effective on hard rock, but its use was limited because of a notorious lack of durability. Nevertheless, the mechanical rock drill could outwork the best double jack teams in existence — barring breakdowns.

Burleigh redesigned the drill and patented the improvement himself. These first "Burleighs" were 350-pound behemoths with 80 moving parts and manufactured at a cost of $400 each. They were introduced to western hardrock mining in June, 1870, at the camp of Silver Plume in the Georgetown, Colorado, mining district. Before a crowd of curious miners, the steam-powered Burleigh was turned loose on the hard rock of Sherman Mountain in a tunnel which, in time, would be named in honor of the drill and its inventor — the Burleigh Tunnel. With a hissing boiler outside the portal and a crudely insulated hose conducting steam to the Burleigh, the deafening thunder of a rock drill reverberated inside a Colorado mountain for the first time. Although there remained great room for improvement on that first drill, it was a sound that would never stop.

The most obvious problem of the drill in hardrock use was the steam itself. Steam expended in powering the piston was exhausted directly into the underground confines, creating unbearable heat and humidity and totally obscuring vision. Hoses were another problem. Since steam could not be generated in the underground, loss of heat and energy increased with the length of the poorly insulated hose connecting the distant boiler and the drill. At the drill itself, the weakest points were the flexible hoses which ruptured with distressing frequency to instantly scald the miners.

Among the miners who bore witness to that first Colorado underground trial of the Burleigh was a young man named J. George Leyner. A hardrock miner himself, Leyner knew too well the rigors of hand steel drilling, and recognized the potential and limitations of Burleigh's rock drill. After a few more years of sweating over hammers and hand steels in the underground, Leyner left the mines to study engineering. In 1877 he returned to Colorado with a design for a threaded bar which imparted an automatic rotary action to the

34

steel. His rotation device greatly increased the effectiveness of the mechanical drill, an accomplishment that would be overshadowed by an infinitely more significant improvement to the drill George Leyner would make twenty-five years later.

Improvements on the Burleigh drill brought its weight down to a more manageable 240 pounds. All the drills were converted to more practical compressed air power and shipped to Nevada's Comstock Lode for real testing in driving the Sutro Tunnel. Again, the drills proved effective on hard rock but were still plagued by poor durability. Five drills were required to keep one running continuously. The cutting edges of the drill steels, caught between the vicious pounding of the drill and the hard rock, never lasted beyond two feet of hole. Replacing the dulled steels was not a simple matter since the steel and the drill piston were one unit. Drifts were filled with "nippers" hauling loads of dulled steels and broken drill parts to the shaft stations, then returning with reformed, sharpened steel-piston units and other replacement parts.

Improvement in durability came slowly, for the steel used in manufacturing the drills was subjected to the severest mechanical stresses man had yet devised. True reliability would have to wait until alloying technology caught up with that of the drills themselves. Improvement in other areas continued. In 1875, a drill steel separate from the piston was designed, now letting the miner change a dulled steel in a few seconds. The enormous volume of exhausted air from the drills also aided ventilation. Even though it was laden with an oil mist, anything was better than the usual stale, oxygen-depleted air of the underground.

In use, the miner mounted the drills on vertical or horizontal steel columns jacked securely between the rock of the drifts. A universal joint which slid along the column could also angle and pivot, thus allowing the miner to drill any desired pattern of holes. Barring breakdowns, the miner and his partner could drill out a four-foot hole, depending on the hardness of the rock, in about five minutes — ten times faster than an expert double jack team. The miners working the drills were now obliged to stuff rags in their ears for protection from the roar that echoed through the underground. While the miners were concerned about their ears, they were totally unaware of the real hazard — the white cloud of rock dust that poured from every hole the wonderful new drills made.

But the drills substantially reduced labor costs and development time in the underground. Mine owners were overjoyed; if they believed in God, they thanked him profusely for Burleigh's drill; if not, they celebrated their joy with more secular excesses. The double jack teams, which had been the largest part of a mine owner's labor cost, were laid off by the hundreds. In their place, the owners were delighted to hire a slightly smaller army of blacksmiths to keep up with the day-long job of resharpening drill steels. Miners now tripled their output, receiving for their efforts exactly the same pay and another load of resharpened steels to dull. Sweating and cursing in the flickering candlelight alongside the heavy, greasy drills, miners soon learned they could drill six-foot-deep holes and, using giant powder, "pull" the entire face. Drifts that once crept through hard rock now advanced by leaps and bounds. Although hand drilling would remain in use for many decades, especially in smaller mines on shoestring budgets, any owner with financial backing and an ore body worth mining built the heart of his operation around a steam-driven air compressor and the mechanical rock drill.

In 1876, Colorado graduated from territorial status to statehood, thanks to a renewed economic life based almost entirely on mining. Denver was growing into a mine equipment manufacturing center; steam engines had been built there since 1870, and by 1875, several factories were turning out stamp mills, steam winches, pumps, and ore cars. The capital city was becoming the major supply and logistical center for most of the Rocky Mountain mining industry. Colorado was prepared for the rapid development of its hardrock mining industry; all it needed was a grand silver strike.

When that grand strike was made at Leadville, the subsequent development of the mining district and the city was astonishing. Growth was limited only by the speed of mule trains and freight wagons hauling supplies over the mountain passes. While a few of the first wagons brought such superfluous niceties as pianos, most were laden with the hardware and materials to build mines and the city. Long lines of wagons creaked under heavy loads of crated rock drills and their replacement parts, bundles of drill steels, tons of giant powder, reels of newly introduced wire rope, long lengths of pipe, thousands of shovels, picks, saws, rails, ore buckets, ore cars, steam boilers, Ingersoll air compressors, and equipment to be installed in mills and smelters not yet built. Never before had a mining district and its serving city developed as rapidly as Leadville. Even as the

36

mountains of equipment were offloaded on the muddy streets, the rumble of giant powder blasts from the direction of Fryer, Carbonate, and Iron Hills reported the advance of shafts and drifts. Every day, it seemed, another working blasted through to silver ore, not simply paying ore, but bonanza mineral. Claims were already staked from the streets of Leadville right up to the Mosquito Range.

The press made the best of the Leadville rush, printing glowing accounts of the silver fortunes waiting to be made. A man could "set himself up" in Leadville, so it was said, for a mere $100 to purchase the simple necessities which included heavy clothes (after all, Leadville was located at the "invigorating" elevation of 10,000 feet and possessed a "refreshing" mountain climate), hand steels, hammers, candles, and even scales (presumably to conveniently weigh the silver as it was picked from the rock). The press succeeded admirably both in selling newspapers and inducing many to leave their homes all over the country to help populate Colorado and Leadville.

The "$100 set up" idea may have had some merit a few years before, but not in 1878 when the independent hardrock miner was already at a serious disadvantage to the well-financed consolidated interests. Speed of exploration was of vital importance. Most Leadville lode claims were staked not on discovery, but on the fervent hope that mineral existed in the rock below. In strict legal terms, however, the act of positive mineral discovery superceded a prior claim. The $100 miner could be sinking his exploratory shaft on his claim at a snail's pace, while the underground workings of the consolidated on the adjacent claims, led by the thundering rock drills, might "discover" his silver ore body. If an independent miner did make a strike, there was no alternative but to sell out or join a consolidated mining company which had the financial resources to afford the necessary and expensive hardrock tools for rapid development and efficient production. The miner's opportunity now lay not in discovery and production of his own mine, but only in discovery.

In the excitement of the rush, it took only months for the mining district to become a hopeless jumble of claims. Thousands of claims were quickly staked and recorded, among them legal claims, counter claims, superimposing claims, and jumped claims, all of which were further confused by highly suspect surveying procedures. It was little wonder that Leadville soon hosted the largest population of lawyers in the state.

Many fortunes were made or lost in the chaotic wheeling and

dealing of the early months of 1878. Lucky strikes, saltings, misrepresentations, claim jumpings, grubstakes, and precise timing in purchasing and selling, together with other unpredictable events, made the difference between success and failure, between becoming an employer or an employee. The classic demonstration of the role luck played in mining fortunes was the case of Horace Austin Warner Tabor.

In 1878, Tabor, the old California Gulch placer miner and now storekeeper, was already forty-seven years old. His moderate placer mining success and his wife's considerable business acumen had long established him as the leading Oro City merchant. When attention turned from gold to silver, Tabor moved his store down the gulch to the site of the developing new town, Leadville. Tabor's wealth was then about $35,000, a very respectable sum that permitted the storekeeper to gamble a bit on the luck of the hardrock prospectors that scoured the hills.

Two of those prospectors, August Rische and George Hook, both shoemakers by trade and both broke, appealed to Tabor's recognized grubstaking generosity. An equal partnership was formed in April, 1878; Rische and Hook, both honest, hardworking men, would do the prospecting, while Tabor would provide the groceries and supplies. Tabor's initial contribution amounted to $17. As Tabor tended to his business, Rische and Hook sank a narrow shaft with hand steels on their Little Pittsburg claim. When groceries ran low, the two miners would pay a visit to Tabor. And when the shaft progressed deeper, the merchant also provided a hand winch and wheelbarrow. After one month, Tabor's total investment in the partnership was $64.

By mid-May, the tiny shaft was sunk past twenty feet. Day after day, Hook and Rische pounded the hand steels and laboriously hauled out the blasted rock in buckets. On a good day, they sank their shaft another foot, removing two or three tons of rock in the process. At day's end, the fuses would be ignited and the last man would climb the rickety ladder to the surface. By morning, the smoke and fumes would be long dissipated and work could begin again.

The shaft had reached twenty-five feet when, on a fine May morning, the first man down the ladder found not the usual country rock in the muckpile, but a black crystalline mineral. The assay report was beyond their highest hopes. The Little Pittsburg ore body, discovered at a material cost of $64, contained 50% lead and 300 ounces of silver per ton. One week later, the Little Pittsburg had produced $8,000.

Within a month, production had been expanded to ten tons per day. Every day, the ore buckets brought to the surface over 2,000 ounces of silver.

The original Little Pittsburg partnership did not last long thereafter. A $10,000 dividend was declared among the three partners; then, in September, George Hook sold out to Rische and Tabor for $90,000. A month later August Rische, who would never resole another shoe in his life, sold out to Tabor and an associate for $265,000.

Tabor had expended very little of his mining luck in the Little Pittsburg venture. Adjacent to that property, William "Chicken Bill" Lovell was working to duplicate the feat of Rische and Hook. After sweating over the hand steels to sink a shaft twenty feet without success on his Chrysolite claim, Chicken Bill decided there must be an easier way. He quietly appropriated some of the Little Pittsburg's high grade ore, dumped it down his own shaft, and let it flood. A short time later, he had his "samples" assayed. The results, naturally, were most impressive. In July, 1878, he sold his salted Chrysolite property to Tabor for a reported $10,000. Even though the truth was soon learned, Tabor hired a team of miners to sink the unproductive shaft deeper. After working their way only ten feet deeper, Tabor's miners blasted their way into lead-silver ore rivaling that of the Little Pittsburg. Chicken Bill's first laugh was worth a quick $10,000; Tabor's last laugh, over a year and a half later, amounted to a million and a half.

The Little Pittsburg was a tremendous producer, but only over a brief two-year period. Tabor's luck continued unabated; after profiting enormously, he sold out, just before the mine exhausted, for another million. But Tabor had yet to be a sole owner of a mine. To satisfy himself, he bought the Matchless for $117,000. His miners took nearly one year to get the mine into production, but it, too, proved well worth the effort. The Matchless brought Tabor an average of $2,000 every day and its best ore assayed to 10,000 ounces of silver per ton.

H. A. W. Tabor became synonymous with silver and Leadville. A generous and popular man, his silver carried him first to Mayor of Leadville, then to Lieutenant Governor of Colorado, and even to the United States Senate. Tabor went on to build opera houses and grand hotels, and would be remembered in the history books as a "silver baron," never as the placer miner who once sweated over a shovel in the mud of California Gulch for a couple of ounces of gold per day. But, then, that was the way of history and those who recorded it; it was always the gold and the silver, never the men who mined it.

Leadville's spectacular growth in 1878 and 1879 was backed by the production of extraordinarily rich silver ore. The richest mine of them all, at least over one short, well-documented period, was the Robert E. Lee, one of the prime properties on celebrated Fryer Hill. After encountering some particularly rich ore in 1879, the owners decided to see just how much the mine could produce over a twenty-four-hour period. Hoist trouble put a premature end to the effort, but after seventeen hours, the Robert E. Lee's miners had produced ore valued at an astounding $118,500. The richest ore mined that memorable day assayed to 11,000 ounces of silver per ton; half the overall weight of the mined ore was actually silver.

By January, 1880, thanks to an 1879 mine production of $10,000,000, Leadville had grown into a major city the other Colorado silver camps could only look up to with envy. A commemorative article in a January, 1880 Leadville newspaper recapped the "history" of the city, listing proudly the large number of banks, stores, hotels, mines, smelters, and other notable establishments, concluding that Leadville had already achieved the heights of social, civil, and economic development. Leadville was a fairly well-balanced industrial system boasting a population of 20,000 where only a few hundred had been present three years earlier. Unlike Oro City, a man could now specialize in one of many occupations; employment opportunities abounded in mining, smelting, freight and transportation, construction, storekeeping, bartending, assaying, lumbering, and in the growing municipal fire and police services. Booming mine production and the continuing stream of capital from the East seemed to assure the future. Stock in the Leadville mines, whether the mine existed or not, sold nationally as fast as the certificates could be printed. Only two years old, Leadville had all the businesses and services enjoyed by older, more mature cities.

Leadville may have matured economically and industrially, but it did so without the advantage of an orderly, measured development in which problems could be identified, solutions proposed, and logical decisions made. Accompanying the constructive employment opportunities were others even more lucrative in prostitution, gambling, bunko, thievery, and simple "leeching," practiced by many who found the pickings in Leadville far superior to those in lesser camps. True

40

community interest was rare; most people came to Leadville for the express purpose of making a fortune, or at least more money than they could elsewhere, and not to waste their energy on personally unproductive civic endeavors. From the beginning, it was inevitable that grave problems in sanitation, health, transportation, services, and law and order would prevail.

Basic growth occurred so quickly that attention was already turning to construction of opera houses and gaslight systems; assurance, perhaps, for the affluent that they were indeed living in a civilized world. Such superfluous trappings appealed to journalists whose words and opinions shaped the outside image of Leadville. With a bit of enhancement that was within the journalistic guidelines of the era, Leadville's civic, social, and economic adventures were colorfully reported to the East and Europe; and the booming city remained an El Dorado for fortune seekers, a glamorous mecca to which solid citizens and scoundrels beat a steady path.

The few unflattering reports of Leadville usually appeared in newspapers of rival mining camps, notably Deadwood, which frequently mentioned the violence, depravity, and serious health problems of the two-mile-high city. Such reports were most often discounted as a sour grapes reaction to Leadville's stunning rise to fame and fortune that had stolen publicity and investment potential from the other camps. The general public in the United States and Europe wanted to read of a glamorous Leadville, and the press would see that they did.

Many injustices of history may be attributed to favoritism, ignorance, and prejudice in journalism, and hardrock mining is a valid example. Every aspect of Leadville was covered repeatedly, with the exception of the hardrock miner and his work. This disinterest in mining was not always the case; the early placer miners of the gold rushes had great appeal to journalists as romantic figures seeking fortunes in a very visible and easily understood manner. But now in the hardrock era, the miner was hidden in a mysterious underground world where even his simplest operations were described in a strange and specialized vocabulary. Journalists stayed clear of the darkness and danger of the mines, and few, if any, miners were serious writers. In the end, the mines and miners were forgotten. It sufficed to say a shaft had been sunk and rich ore struck. Journalists could then return to the more appealing and comprehensible stories of silver barons, opera houses, and gaslight systems. In future history books,

Hardrock mining in the 1880s was a curious transition of the old and the new. Here, the time-honored ore bucket is powered by a new steam-powered hoist. Both headframe and hoist room are enclosed in the same structure. The potential danger to a miner riding the bucket within the narrow confines of the shaft is apparent.

Colorado Historical Society

it would seem that Leadville's silver appeared by magic. In 1880, nearly one-third of the city's population was engaged in some aspect of mining, and it was their achievements, glamorous or not, that built Leadville.

The shafts and portals were the demarcation line separating the conventional world from the world of the hardrock miner; it was there the historians and journalists stopped while the miner, with his drill steels and candles, continued. On his shift the first thing the miner saw was the mine shaft, and that was the beginning of ten or twelve hours filled with constant danger. Iron buckets the size of large barrels were shaft carry-all vehicles; they lowered men, sharpened drill steels, and supplies, then raised men, dulled drill steels, and, hopefully, paying ore. Without guides to stabilize their vertical descent, nor any automatic braking device to halt accidental free-fall descents, the buckets offered a wild, lurching ride that too often spilled both materials and men. The early Leadville newspapers covered the mines primarily from the financially-related standpoints of production, ore reserves, and profits. The only other aspects of underground mining to warrant mention in the newspapers, interestingly enough, were the macabre accidents that occurred daily. The shafts, being the most dangerous part of early hardrock mines, provided the journalist with ample opportunity, for the miner had no way of knowing how a simple descent down the shaft might end. The following news excerpts are only a few of those that appeared during a nine-month period in 1879-80.

TWO MEN DROPPED DOWN A SHAFT

TWO MEN DROPPED 200 FEET AND ARE BADLY INJURED

One of those shocking accidents that seem to be indispensable in mining camps and accompanied with great pain if not loss of life occurred yesterday on the Blind Tom Lode of Carbonate Hill. . . . when suddenly the brake of the whim broke and the bucket with its human cargo was sent to the bottom at a terrific rate. . . .

A BAD BRAKE

THE BRAKE OF A WHIM IS BROKEN AND A MAN DROPS 200 FEET

Another serious accident occurred last night and should be a warning to all miners that they cannot be too careful with their appliances, especially with their hoisting apparatus. . . .

DROWNED

John Doonan drowned yesterday in the Cyclops Mine by falling down a shaft into a body of water. Mechanical failure of the windlass. . . .

KILLED IN A MINE

MEETS DEATH AT BOTTOM OF SHAFT

. . . the wire cable which proved to be very defective because of the constant use parted, the heavy bucket shot down the shaft striking the unfortunate miner on the head and crushing his skull. . . .

A TERRIBLE LEAP

Thomas Gardner, a Miner, fell a distance of 90 feet to his death when a windlass failed. . . .

ANOTHER MINE ACCIDENT

DEATH CAUSED BY FALL OF 36 FEET

Another life has been lost by one of those horrible accidents common in mining countries and which it appears cannot be prevented. Two miners, being lowered to their duties, were suddenly pitched from a swinging bucket. . . .

44

Mechanical failure of hoists in the shafts caused most accidents, but not all. Merely being close to a mine shaft was dangerous, especially in the poor light, and even when all the equipment functioned perfectly.

DOWN SHAFT
THOMAS O'MALLEY MEETS DEATH AT BOTTOM OF SHAFT

Another fatal accident in the mines occurred yesterday when a miner grew dizzy, lost his footing and fell the distance of 170 feet. . . .

80 FEET WAS THE DISTANCE TRAVELED BY A MINER ON HIS WAY FROM LIFE TO DEATH
ANOTHER TERRIBLE ACCIDENT IN THE ERIE No. 1 MINE

And still another terrible accident has occurred in this vicinity which adds yet another name to the long list of those who have suffered unexpected deaths. . . . apparently unaware that he had reached the shaft, [the miner] fell, and unable to hold himself, plummeted. . . .

The miner soon learned that the rapidly increasing mechanization of shafts and hoists worsened the accident rates. When steam power was brought to a mine, tall headframes were erected with large sheave wheels to convey the hoist cable from the powerful steam winch into the shaft. And as load capacity and speed increased, the miner faced greater danger than ever in riding the buckets. To alleviate the problem, shaft cages were designed to run along timber guides. This stabilized the cage, but the miner risked crushed arms and legs if a limb should be caught between the open cage and the shaft timbers. Neither the shaft nor the cage had safety features, so

45

the ultimate responsibility for life and death was in the hands of the hoist operator, who sat comfortably in the hoist shack to the rear of the headframe, judging the position of the cage within the shaft by crude indicator devices measuring the length of cable displaced from the winch drum. Not only were the hoistmen subject to human error, they were generally ill-trained and prone to distraction while the hoist was in operation. Most accidents occurred within the shaft, but the hoistman's ultimate error was failing to stop the ascending cage at the collar, thus running it into the sheave wheel, breaking the cable, and triggering another fatal accident. Hoistmen were informed of desired cage movement by bell signals. This created more trouble since no standard code existed; each mine adopted its own system and, since miners changed jobs frequently, confusion was rampant. There was no limit to the ways in which death could claim a miner in the shafts. A wrench, for example, accidentally dropped down a shaft could easily gather sufficient speed to kill a miner working at the bottom.

Candle flames rarely survived the air drafts in a shaft, and most ascents and descents were made in darkness. The miner began his shift crowded together with his partners in the open cages awaiting the stomach-wrenching lurch that started his noisy, clattering descent. The miner saw each passing level station as an eerie glow of yellow light shrouded in the haze of dust, smoke, and fumes that lingered from the blasting of the previous shift. When he reached his working level, the first task facing the miner "coming on" was mucking. Working with a shovel "off the sheet," he filled a one-ton ore car, then pushed it to the shaft station along the light, eighteen-inch rails. Ore cars were first moved manually, or hand trammed, but after expansion of the workings, mules were used for haulage.

By 1880, the Leadville mines used hundreds of mules in the growing maze of underground workings. With greater perception than they are usually credited with, the animals displayed little cooperation and enthusiasm when their time came to descend into the shafts. Each mule had to be securely tied and slung to prevent it from injuring or even killing itself, or from kicking the sides of the shaft loose during the descent. Upon arrival in the underground, the mules were dragged onto the level and kept tied for hours to accustom them slowly to their new environment. Untying revealed not a furious animal ready to tear the drifts apart, but a docile, easily-led beast of burden already resigned to the dark, claustrophobic, and muted

When mines became too extensive to rely upon hand tramming, the job of underground haulage fell to mules. In many instances the animals were literally worked to death, and removed from the underground only after they were physically incapable of pulling the endless strings of ore cars. The miners are employing oil lamps attached to their caps for light. The overhead pipe conveys compressed air to the drills.

atmosphere of the underground. That mule could now fully expect to spend its entire career, which often meant its life, in the "hole." By 1900, the Leadville mines had "twenty-year seniority" mules which had not once during that time seen the light of day. They had spent all those years tethered to an ore car and, during their endless labor in the dark shafts, had gone totally blind. Since drills were expensive and mules were cheap, it is not likely the animals enjoyed any enviable position on the evacuation list in the event of fire or flood in the underground. The mules' abundant droppings enhanced the already distinctive fragrance of the mines. Mingled with the oil mist from the drills, the fumes and smoke from giant powder, the rotting, mildewed timbers, and the human waste of the miners themselves which, in the 1880s, was deposited alongside that of the mules, it created an aromatic essence of noteworthy and lasting character.

When the heading was mucked out, the miner and his partner

47

turned to timbering. Square-set timbering, a system which had originated in the Cornish tin mines, was already standard in the West. It was based upon series of "sets," each constructed of two nearly-vertical posts and bridged by a third timber of equal girth, usually eight inches square. The sets were installed at fixed intervals of several feet and cribbed upwards to the back, then wedged firmly in place. As the drift advanced, the miner "tied in" each new timber set to the previous set, using lighter braces and overhead planks, or "lagging," which helped keep the smaller, loose rock off his head. If the rock became "poor," or prone to "pay off," the distance between sets was shortened to increase their support. Naturally, from the standpoint of time and expense, mine owners wished to install the least timber possible. Safety was never a consideration, as long as the drift remained open and operational. Still, timber use was prodigious and entire forests ended up in the underground. Leadville's underground workings soon totalled over 100 miles and most were supported with timber. The mine requirements were the base for a large, profitable timber industry for the duration of the silver boom.

As he worked, the miner had to always be alert for fire, since the well-timbered workings and open flame light sources were a serious hazard. Candles were less of a hazard than the brighter oil lamps. If knocked over, a candle probably would not cause a catastrophe, but an oil lamp might. Mine timbers were either rotting in water or tinder dry, and a spill of flaming oil could turn the underground into a holocaust in minutes. The ultimate danger of underground fire was not flames, heat, or eventual destruction of timber support, but rapid consumption of oxygen and generation of highly poisonous carbon monoxide. The small shafts precluded rapid evacuation and miners could die on the lower levels before the cage ever appeared to hoist them to safety. The Leadville mines fortunately remained free of any mass fire-related deaths, unlike the neighboring silver camp of Aspen. There, at the turn of the century, fourteen miners, unable to reach the surface during a fire at the Union-Smuggler Mine, suffocated to death.

As the mines increased in both size and complexity, the miner found his health and safety were governed not only by his actions, but more and more by others over whom he had little control. Hoistmen were the leading example, but in the intertwining underground labyrinths of the Leadville district, this relationship even spread between different mines. It was no secret that one company's work-

48

ings might "inadvertently" wander into the legal ground of another company. Such incursions were usually in knowing, zealous pursuit of a good vein of mineral; legality was a moot point, ore was ore, and it all smelted down to silver metal. When miners drove into another company's workings, the event could be celebrated in two ways: either by sharing cigarettes with the other miners, or by swinging axes with intent to commit the greatest bodily harm possible.

One such instance turned to tragedy. In 1880, miners of the Little Chief and the Chrysolite left their breakthrough point open as part of a common ventilation system. Several weeks later, an underground fire roared through the Chrysolite. Before the Little Chief would shut down its ventilation system to aid in extinguishing the stubborn blaze, a court order was necessary. The Little Chief managers grudgingly complied, but when the fire could not be quickly extinguished, they began to fret over their lost production time and profits. Finally, in defiance of the court order, they reopened the vent system to resume mining. When the draft swept into the Chrysolite workings, the smoldering embers flared again and two Chrysolite miners fighting the fire suffocated to death.

The Chrysolite-Little Chief incident clearly demonstrated the pressures brought to bear upon mine supervisors by owners and capitalists seeking to protect or increase profits on their huge investments. However far removed they were from the mines, their incessant demands for greater production dictated the pace of every mine operation. If other Leadville mines were producing fortunes daily, the mine they backed damned well better produce one, too. And if it didn't, or if production slowed unacceptably, there would be hell to pay on the part of a supervisor. Careers as well as capital were on the line, and so were the professional reputations of engineers and supervisors, even the pride of the capitalists. Throughout every Leadville mine, the order was always for more ore, and damned how the miners got it.

With timbering completed, the face was ready for drilling, and the miner and his partner dragged the columns and drills forward. They jacked and wedged the column in place, then bolted the drill to the universal joint, attached the air hose, and readied the stack of drill steels. As the miner opened an air valve to fill the hose, the drill began hissing and sputtering. He inserted a short "starter" steel, then advanced the drill along its threaded travel bar until the cutting edge of the steel touched the rock face. When his gloved hand

49

slammed the single valve control open, the silence was shattered in thunderous concussions as the steel viciously attacked the rock. The cloud of white rock dust quickly filled the heading, swirling wildly on the streams of vented air that rushed from the drill. Through the eerie mist came pieces of falling rock, jarred loose by the deafening roar that made even shouted words impossible to understand. Steel quickly disappeared into the rock as the miner manually cranked the screw advancement at the rear of the drill. A brief moment of sudden and strange silence prevailed as the driller's partner changed the steel to one of longer length. Again the driller slammed the drill valve forward, and again the terrible din erupted as the new steel bit ever deeper into the rock. As nippers appeared to haul away the growing pile of dulled steels, blacksmiths on the surface heated and hammered to reform the cutting edges. And in the underground, the miners sweated and swore beside the thundering drill, coughing and hacking in the cloud of white rock dust.

Rock dust was not the only problem faced in drilling. Another was the rash of eye injuries from flying rock particles. Of a far more deadly nature was the occasional explosion of the drill itself, an occurrence finally traced to the explosive compression-temperature effect on the lubricating oil mist within the drill cylinder, similar to the firing principle of the diesel engine. But in the 1880s, the real tragedy of the drills was still unknown, although miners had begun to question the effect of the rock dust upon their lungs.

Drills continued to improve; by 1882, their weight had been reduced to 220 pounds. Six eastern manufacturers shipped them by the trainload to the booming mines of the Rockies. Not only had their durability improved, but more efficient, mass manufacturing techniques reduced the price, making the drills more attractive than ever to mine owners. Small mines still used the old hand steels, but the sound of progress in the mining West was the thunder of the mechanical rock drill.

After the hour-long job of drilling out a seven-foot-square face, the miners dismounted the drill from the column, dragged both back, and brought up the giant powder. Giant was still extremely hazardous, a fact belied by the ease and apparent confidence with which the miners handled it. Thermal instability caused by the fifty-two degree freezing temperature of nitroglycerin remained the greatest danger. And in the highest valley of the Arkansas, that magic temperature was noted every single morning, season notwithstanding. Frozen

50

*A classic, rare photograph of two early hardrock miners and their
widowmaker drill. This drill, probably about 1880, weighed over 300 pounds
and, in operation, filled the miners' heading with a deafening thunder beyond
description. The introduction of the mechanical rock drill was the greatest
single advancement in hardrock mining, but while mine development time
was dramatically reduced, the drills churned up clouds of rock dust which
caused silicosis in thousands of miners and one of the greatest tragedies in
American industry.*
Denver Public Library—Western History Department

Montrose Library District
434 S. 1st St
Montrose, CO

giant was simple to detect if one took the time to unwrap the paper cartridges and look; the normally pasty material would be covered by a delicate latticework of long, white crystals. Those pretty crystals were pure nitroglycerin, every bit as shock sensitive as the feared liquid. In the frozen, separated state, it was absurd to attempt to transport giant, much less to tamp it in place in a drill hole. To make it safely usable again, the frozen giant had to be thawed.

Thawing was not a simple matter of heating, for the sensitivity increased even further during thermal change. At the actual point of physical transition from a solid back to a liquid, the sensitivity became extreme. Thawing required laboratory equipment as well as the most delicate touch. Most unfortunately, the miners had neither. For "laboratory equipment," they relied upon the cast iron wood burning stoves in their small, crowded cabins. Accordingly, the miners achieved only mixed success in thawing giant.

KILLED BY GIANT POWDER

EXPLOSION WHILE HEATING IT

Late yesterday afternoon, a corpse was taken to Undertaker Roger's establishment.... The dead man ... was found to be in terrible condition with his entire body perforated with holes where the stones around the fire had been thrown into him....

EXPLOSION

TWO MEN SERIOUSLY INJURED WHILE HEATING GIANT POWDER

Notwithstanding the numerous accidents that have occurred in this vicinity as of late, there are those who do not take heed and who continue to handle explosives without care and at risk of their lives. A case of this kind occurred yesterday ... at the Penfield Mine in South Evans. While two men were engaged in the dangerous task of melting Hercules powder over a stove, the explosive composition ignited in some manner and a terrific explosion followed immediately....

EXPLOSION

ANOTHER PREMATURE EXPLOSION
OF POWDER CARTRIDGES

Yesterday morning an explosion of nitroglycerin took place, causing yet another miner to suffer indescribable pain. He was warming three sticks of giant powder in the oven of a sheet iron stove a short distance from the mouth of the tunnel. He placed the explosive inside the stove, then sat down to wait its warming, and when he thought it had become sufficiently heated he attempted to remove them. A terrible explosion ensued. . . . The stove of course was blown to atoms. . . .

For all the injuries and deaths that came from thawing giant powder, there were many more narrow escapes. One group of miners were playing poker in their cabin as a few sticks of giant thawed atop their stove. One miner fortunately chanced to glance up from his hand to note with appropriate concern that the giant was indeed thawing — in fact it was on fire. The miners hastily evacuated the steamy cabin, and as they fled through waist-deep snow in their long underwear, their cabin was blown apart in what the newspapers called a "cataclysmic" explosion, one that included the unopened cases of giant stored beneath their bunks. Most large mines wisely maintained heated powder houses where giant was kept ready for use without going through the thawing process.

Hundreds of times each day throughout the district, the miners prepared their drilled-out faces for blasting. They tamped each stick of giant firmly in place, leaving the single fuse dangling from each hole. Preparing the fuse and blasting cap properly was also of great importance, for a loose crimp could cause a misfire. After the miner lit the fuses, he quickly retreated, hopefully, to safety. Considering the uncertain operation of the hoists, that was not always the case.

A TERRIBLE ACCIDENT

MAN FALLS 60 FEET THEN IS BLOWN UP BY BLAST

. . . At 12:00 noon, John Duhen, one of the workmen, had just lighted a fuse for a blast and placing one foot in the bucket, called for the men above to hoist. He ascended 60 feet from the bottom of shaft when one of the standards of the windlass broke. It fell across the shaft and there caught, but the sudden fall of about six feet threw Duhen from the bucket and he fell 60 feet to the bottom of the shaft. Within a minute thereafter, the blast went off. The windlass was righted and a man lowered, but upon reaching the bottom, the injured man was found to be beyond help. . . .

Some accidents were cruel and ironic, for a miner escaping from one danger could fall victim to another.

FATAL FALL

MINER FALLS 165 FEET TO DEATH
But Falls On Fuse To Prevent Being Blown Up

. . . but certainly would have been killed if he had survived his terrible fall. . . .

Even if there were no overt accidents or equipment malfunctions, the mines still made no allowance for inevitable, simple human inattentiveness.

BLOWN UP

ANOTHER MINE EXPLOSION MAIMS MINER

One of those unforeseen events which do not cast their shadows before and are

54

becoming a frequent occurrence in and around this city was reported yesterday in the Glass Mine in the Pendry Consolidation on Carbonate Hill. John McGinnis, a miner, was preparing a blast and was holding the cap in one hand and a candle in the other. As he was thus engaged, the fuse accidentally came into contact with the candle and ignited without his knowledge, he being engaged at the time with his comrade in labor, Austin Cavanaugh. The fuse ignited quite close to the cap and before either party were aware of the terrible danger they were in, an explosion took place which hurled both men some distance from the scene of the accident. . . .

Even if all went well, there always remained the question of whether the round would detonate; more importantly, whether *all* of it would detonate. Misfires, the failure of at least one charge in the round to detonate, could be caused by any number of things such as manufacturing defects in the caps or detonation of the first charge extinguishing the fuses of the later charges. A defective fuse or misfired cap might retain a live spark for hours and be capable of detonating a charge without warning at any time.

BLOWN UP
ANOTHER PAINFUL ACCIDENT IN ONE OF THE MINES

. . . and when he returned to check upon the failure of the blast, it went off. . . .

ACCIDENT IN A MINE
HE RETURNS TO MEET BLAST

. . . the blast not occurring as soon as he thought it should, he advanced toward it to remedy the defect. When he reached the spot, the charge exploded, blowing him a considerable distance and tearing off his right hand. . . .

55

BLOWN UP

The miner counted each separate detonation in his timed round very carefully, listening for the gap in the sequence of concussions that might indicate a possible misfire. Misfires were distressingly frequent, and the combination of misfired caps or powder together with the mechanical drills was deadly. Many miners were killed or maimed by unknowingly drilling into a misfire or by using a drill to attempt to remove one.

ANOTHER EXPLOSION

The sheer number of mine deaths and injuries seemed to exhaust the copy originality of the Leadville *Herald* writer, yet he was still able to muster a touch of sarcasm when needed.

56

ANOTHER EXPLOSION

TWO MEN SEVERELY INJURED IN SILVER CHORD MINE

For several weeks past, the number of accidents among the mines have been relatively few; in fact several of the surgeons about town have been heard to complain that their businesses have been becoming terribly thin and that they should soon be obliged to seek new fields of labor. But the dull monotony has at last been broken, first by the caving of the Denver City shaft, and again yesterday by an explosion at the Silver Chord Mine on Iron Hill . . . the miner endeavored to take out an unexploded charge with a drill. . . .

The last thing the miner did on his ten- or twelve-hour shift was blast. The time between his departure and the arrival of his counterpart on the next shift would permit at least some of the smoke, fumes, gases, and dust to clear, although the poor ventilation was another hazard the miner faced.

DEATH FROM INHALING GIANT POWDER

. . . he had been a miner by occupation and for the last five weeks had been confined to his cabin in consequence of inhaling giant smoke powder in the mines. . . .

After the miner faced the dangers of the shafts, hoists, drills, and giant powder, there was still the problem of falling rock.

CAVED IN

A SHAFT GIVES WAY
A Terrible Death Is Suffered
By Mr. Gorham Foster

Once again, the *Herald* is called upon to present the account of another appall-

ing accident which was fatal in its results. Without warning, timber and rocks
within a shaft collapsed. . . .

MANGLED IN A MINE
WILLIAM KELLY KILLED AT WORK
IN HOWELL MINE
. . . when a large quantity of rock broke
loose and killed him instantly. . . .

The period from 1878 to 1881 was most dangerous for the miner in
terms of fatalities, not surprisingly since these years were the most
disorganized and pressured. Accurate records of mine fatalities do not
exist prior to November, 1879, but in the seven-month period from
that time through May, 1880, the *Herald* reported twenty-six
fatalities and forty-eight serious injuries, classifying the fatalities by
cause:

Shaft-related 62%
Explosives 26%
Cave-in and Rock Fall 4%
Fumes, Fire, Suffocation..4%
Misc.: Drowning, Crushing...4%

Most of the shaft accidents were directly attributed to some form of
mechanical failure. The greatest hazards were connected with the
new mining innovations that allowed the miner to drill, blast, and
hoist as never before. The 1880s were the peak years of mining's
mechanical revolution; until the engineers were able to control and
tame the innovations they rushed to the mines, it would be the miner
who would pay with life and limb.

Mine deaths, based on reported fatalities, reached forty-two in
1880, then soared to fifty-one, over four per month, in 1881. In 1882, a
significant reduction was noted when "only" twelve died in the Leadville underground. That rate of one mine fatality per month lasted
into the early 1890s. Using these figures as a base, we may estimate
that during Leadville's silver era, 1878 to 1893, approximately 250
miners were killed and twice that number gravely injured. The
actual number is probably higher, since not every fatality, especially
those of the small outlying mines in the higher elevations of the

Mosquito Range, was hauled to town for formal burial and honorable mention in Leadville's newspapers. Since never more than four miners ever died in a single accident, Leadville's good name was spared the stigma of a disaster. The disaster was there, of course but it went unreported, and Leadville's glamorous image remained intact. Leadville's miners simply never died in large enough groups to make their passing noteworthy.

The death and injury rates reflected only the human trauma suffered in accidents. By 1880, when the miner had spent a year or more by the side of his drill, always breathing the cloud of rock dust, he began developing serious lung problems. He became plagued with a racking cough and a worrisome shortness of breath. For lack of a better name, this condition was referred to by doctors as "miners' consumption," a meaningless term that accurately reflected the medical understanding of the problem. Some attributed it to a climatically-aggravated offshoot of the more common tuberculosis since, with the exception of fever and sweating, the symptoms were quite similar. Others, however, surmised that the problem stemmed directly from the inhalation of rock dust. Anyway, the concern was not with miners' coughing, but with how to mine more silver ore. And the best way was by more drilling.

The 1880s attitude regarding mine death and injury was quite simple. It was of little real concern to mine owners and supervisors, except that the loss of experienced miners did tend to slow production. The established legal stand on accidents in the mines, and in United States industry in general, held that: since the worker recognized the risks of the job when he accepted it of his own free will, he alone was responsible for his own health, safety, and life. Furthermore, if a miner became dissatisfied with the job, he was also free to leave. Therefore, mine owners could not be liable for accidents. The first civil suits of wrongful injury and negligence were reversed by the courts and thrown right back at the miners with reasons of "contributory negligence" and "fellow servant liability." Contributory negligence required the injured miner to prove that he himself in some manner had not contributed to his own accident. The reasoning was that if the miner had not been on the cage when the cable parted, he would not have broken his leg. The fellow servant rulings shifted blame from the owner to the other employees, for the owner himself was rarely in the mine when an accident occurred.

Such rulings obligated miners to pay for their own medical costs out of their $3.00 per day wage. Some miners, not able to afford professional medical attention for an injury, simply let their partner perform the required surgery in their cabin. Ugly scars, missing digits, and poorly set bones became a mark of the working miner. Doctors of widely varying education and competence found fertile fields in Leadville as the mines provided a steady stream of mutilated patients. Many insurance companies also saw an opportunity to profit and established convenient agencies in Leadville. One long-running Travelers' Insurance Company advertisement took a direct approach; a caricature of an unfortunate miner was shown plunging down a shaft, below which was printed a long list of miners who had suffered and collected along with graphic descriptions of their injuries.

Jobs in the mines were hardly desirable, yet, in 1880, Leadville was the home of nearly 4,000 miners. Simple economic need drove a man into the mines to collect $3.00 for a ten- or twelve-hour shift. Considering the nature of the work and the risks involved, that wage was gross underpayment and a major factor making possible the owners' enormous profits. Still, compared with most other labor, the miner seemed to do fairly well. Factory and unskilled laborers in the East, if they could even find a job, received only $1.00 per day. Hardrock mining was certainly not the ideal career opportunity, but it did offer the excitement of the mining camps and a chance for the miner to prospect on his own. The miner did exactly that during his free time, sinking prospect holes on abandoned claims and in remote areas still open to claiming. Most areas had already been thoroughly prospected (even today one sees prospect holes above 14,000 feet on the barren peaks of the Sawatch Range), but there was always hope of striking a vein of mineral that would change his life. It had been done before, right there in Leadville, and the miner knew he was on the payroll of a lucky man that did it.

The miners came from every walk of life, but had one common quality. Most were the malcontents, the wanderers, the adventurers, and those who, after the Civil War and the Indian Wars, found a void within themselves aching to be filled with more excitement. Those established financially, however moderately, or those socially content, were not the ones to spend their last dollars rushing to a very uncertain future in the Rockies. The educated, those with civil and refined interests, came out of curiosity. Many took one look at Leadville and left. Leadville was fittingly described in an analogy once

60

drawn between the western mining camps and a twelve-year-old boy who was suddenly given a car and a wallet full of money; he finished "growing" the next year, but was a wild, thirteen-year-old boy who took six men to hold down. Leadville was hard, wild, and ruthless, and most of the men who came to work in the mines had little trouble adapting.

Leadville attracted miners from other camps, but many came directly from the East and Europe where perennially depressed economies provided ample human fuel for frontier expansion. The glowing press reports of the opportunities to be found in Leadville had a special effect on the Cornish and Italians, first-generation immigrants to whom hardrock mining was nothing new. The hardrock techniques developed in the world-famous Cornish tin mines were already standards of the western mines. And twenty years earlier, the Italians pioneered the use of the mechanical rock drill in construction of their spectacular hardrock tunnels beneath the Alps. These groups came specifically to apply their mining skills in a land of grand opportunity and immediately became part of the more stable and respectable elements of the rough Leadville society.

The American emigrants, conversely, exhibited somewhat less feel and respect for mining, considering it a field to conveniently direct their hopes, frustrations, and energies with a minimum of restriction. By 1880, the frontier was already quieting; the military actions were about over, the mountain men were long dead, the big gold strikes had been made, many territories had become states, and more civilization and order moved west every day. The frontier itself would soon be history. And many young men still bursting with raw, undirected energy found hardrock mining a convenient outlet. There was always $3.00 per day available in Leadville, risk and danger enough to satisfy even the most reckless interests, and great social turmoil with its inherent opportunities that a man with wit and courage could capitalize upon. For all these reasons, Leadville never suffered from a shortage of miners.

Among the new arrivals came a man whose adventuring credentials were second to none. As a young man, he had fought in the Civil War under Admiral David Farragut. Then he came west, joining the throngs of men he had fought both alongside and against. The West was truly young then and it was the excitement of the Indian Wars that attracted him. He rejoined the military to serve in a cavalry unit, spending several years as a scout in operations against the Dakota Sioux. In 1877, with the rank of Sergeant, he again left the military. He rode the Overland Stage to Denver where he took a job as a mule skinner, working his way into the Rockies and arriving in Leadville in the spring of 1879.

These months were the peak of the silver rush; the first ore in quantity began to pour from the new mines while thousands of prospectors and miners swarmed over the hills. The mining excitement may have been contagious, for ex-Sergeant Charles J. Senter, Civil War veteran and Indian fighter, decided to try his hand at prospecting. A very independent man, Senter was not inclined to rub shoulders with the frenzied masses; he chose rather to travel to the headwaters of the Arkansas River at Fremont Pass, twelve miles north of the booming city of Leadville. Crossing the Continental Divide to the Ten Mile drainage, he descended below timberline and built a small cabin. Senter then turned to gold prospecting; he panned some color, built his sluices, and soon was successful in washing out enough gold to make a living. From time to time, Senter would leave his sluices and climb above the saddle of Fremont Pass to the barren rock shoulder of Bartlett Mountain.

From the northern part of the Mosquito Range, Bartlett Mountain rises 13,500 feet into the Colorado sky. Somewhere high on the mountain's western slope, even above the point where the first tiny rivulets join to form the Arkansas River, Charles Senter began lode prospecting. Wherever he sank his pick, it seemed, the country rock of weathered granite would yield quickly to a mineral he had never seen before, a white rock laced with black streaks. Those streaks, he noted curiously, rubbed off in the fingers as a dark, greasy stain. Obtaining samples, Senter questioned the composition with other local prospectors, receiving only unknowing shrugs and guesses that leaned toward "some form of graphite." Still, believing the mineral might contain some gold values, Senter staked several claims on Bartlett Mountain.

Charles Senter now held groups of mineral claims that contained a completely unknown, unidentified mineral. To Senter's disappointment, assays revealed no gold at all, and chemists provided no help in identification, most also guessing "some form of graphite." Twenty years earlier, California Gulch miners had a similar experience with a mysterious heavy black mineral that clogged their sluices. Years later it turned out to be the rich lead-silver carbonate mineral that was the foundation of the boom taking place in Leadville at the same time Senter pondered his strange mineral. The lone prospector maintained his claims each year and, using hand steels, even drove a fifty-foot tunnel into the side of the mountain, encountering nothing but that white rock with the black streaks. Whatever that mineral was, Charles Senter had a mountain full of it.

Twelve miles from Fremont Pass and Bartlett Mountain, Leadville roared along on its journey to riches, opening more mines and attracting more miners. Hardrock mining, by its nature, was performed only by strong, young men, or by older men if they were very tough. And if a man was tough when he took a mine job, he was tougher still when he walked out — if he were able to avoid injury and maintain his health. The long underground shifts could be endured only by the rugged, for the deafening noise, heavy physical labor, constant threat of accidents, and the inescapable rash of bruises and lesser injuries sent weaker men to the surface before the end of their first shift. A miner able to last a year became inured to fear of injury or death and accustomed to violence in one form or another. He also became endowed with rippling muscles, calloused hands, and well-scarred knuckles. At the end of his ten or twelve hours underground, he was fit only for drinking, whoring, and fighting, pursuits he found readily available in Leadville. Many historians imply that Leadville's rough and violent image was built on the imported talents of visiting gunslingers and con artists, the Doc Hollidays and Soapy Smiths. Were either of those overly romanticized gentlemen or their contemporaries to engage in a one-on-one, fist-to-fist confrontation with the working miner, my bets would ride with the miner. Most gunslingers were in truth backshooting drunks, and it is unlikely the miner working daily with fulminate caps and giant powder was particularly awed by the threat of firearms. There was indeed violence and death in Leadville, and men did die doubled up on a tobacco-stained barroom floor or in the mud of Harrison Avenue. But most of this celebrated violence in Leadville was caused by the miners themselves, 4,000 of whom shaped the overall tone of life in the city. Still, the total numbers of those beaten or shot to death on the streets were miniscule compared with the human toll of the mines.

Mine conditions and violence painted a grim picture of Leadville, and health problems made it even grimmer. At its alpine elevation, Leadville enjoyed a pleasant, though brief, summer but was cursed

"Rough" was the only word to describe a miner's life – either placer or early hardrock – in Colorado. Cabins were rude and necessarily small to conserve heat in the mountain climate. The Sharps rifle and the fiddle stand out among the rough pine construction and furnishings.

Colorado Historical Society

with a long, bitter winter that made sickness and disease a part of everyday life. The effects of the climate were aggravated by the lifestyle of the residents. Dwellings, even those of the wealthy, were of clapboard; just pine boards nailed over a frame. The popular architectural style was Victorian, emphasizing large, numerous, and elaborate windows that lost huge amounts of heat from already poorly insulated buildings. The community sleeping rooms in the center of the city were little more than drafty sheds; customers of these establishments were those who had arrived in Leadville on their last dollar. If they were dressed in rags when they arrived, they would probably be wearing the same rags when winter set in. Food was available in quantity, if one had the money to pay for it. Meat and grains were the staples; the fresh fruits and vegetables vital to build resistance to the climate and prevailing sickness were expensive and in short supply. Alcohol and drugs, especially morphine and opium, were used in quantities that might make today's ideas of abuse seem mild. Although some of Leadville's residents crawled in stupors into alleys to freeze to death, a more common effect of the lower and middle class Leadville lifestyles was a slow eroding of resistance to disease. Finally, "miners' consumption" left many miners susceptible to other pulmonary diseases.

Epidemics and disease had plagued westward expansion regardless of elevation. Cholera, scarlet fever, meningitis, and diphtheria all affected Leadville, but not with the incidence and severity of pneumonia, tuberculosis, "congestion," and "consumption." Funeral records attribute half of Leadville's deaths to pulmonary problems which collectively overwhelmed the more chronicled and adventurous causes of death such as legal hanging, lynching, shooting, or mine, railroad, and wagon accidents. At the same time, Leadville continued to play upon the "invigorating" local mountain climate, noting proudly and repeatedly that several eastern doctors had recommended the place to patients suffering from pulmonary ailments. In their ignorance, these doctors knew only of the dry, clean air of the Rockies, and nothing of the lifestyles, dwellings, mines, and smelters that made up the real Leadville.

Faced by long and dangerous underground shifts, lower wages than he felt he earned, and a generally depressing environment, it surprised no one when the miner joined his fellows in rudimentary labor organizations, hoping that collective effort might increase his meager portion of Leadville's fortunes. With the help of some labor agitators in the spring of 1880, a group of Fryer Hill miners organized secretly and adopted a list of demands to present to mine owners. The major points were a wage of $4.00 per day and an eight-hour shift. But the miners' attempted labor movement was nothing more than a frustrated reaction to mine work and was backed by little planning or forethought about the possibility of a real strike. They soon learned the power of the Leadville mine owners; not only did the owners refuse to consider the miners' demands, they actually talked of *reducing* wages. In late May, the miners walked off with their partners, first at the Chrysolite and the Little Chief, then at the other mines. Confusion followed when some of the larger mines quickly reopened with scab labor protected by armed guards. Threats and rhetoric were voiced on both sides. Finally, the Governor of Colorado ordered in the militia to protect property. Under martial law, the strikers soon broke and returned to work, their demands unfulfilled. Silver production resumed and Leadville returned to normalcy.

"Normalcy," at this early point in Leadville's silver era, was a changing thing in itself. Undisguised shock followed the announcements by major mines that, unless more high grade mineral was discovered quickly, the extraordinary production levels that Leadville took for granted would not last long. Depletion of the rich ore bodies, never questioned before, was suddenly a very disconcerting topic of conversation. Other changes came with the arrival of the railroad in summer of 1880; prices of food, construction materials, and general supplies declined substantially, while mule skinners sought other employment. Also, in the rickety cars behind the smoking locomotives came a renewed supply of cheap labor, much to the mine owners' pleasure. As early as 1881, several large mines came close to failing, and reluctantly directed their operations to lower grade ore bodies that had been previously bypassed. But new mines were developed to make up the lag in production, and Leadville continued along its course of fortune and fame.

By 1882, all the mine owners had accepted the fact that lower grade ores were the only way the district would sustain itself, and began a much more efficient and orderly system of mining. The pressure to achieve always more production by whatever means necessary was taken off the shoulders of managers and supervisors; emphasis shifted toward a logical engineering approach aimed at the maximum use of ore bodies. This concept was instrumental in a significant reduction in mine fatalities in 1882.

Investment capital, necessary to finance both new mines and expanded operations, was still sought, but the attraction now became the hard facts presented by experienced mining engineers and geologists rather than glowing words of wild-eyed promoters. Even though the enduring excitement shrouded the fact, the city and the mining district had already peaked and were on a long road toward decline. Development continued unabated, however, and when H. A. W. Tabor, now a millionaire many times over, opened his Tabor Grand Hotel on Harrison Avenue, it drew immediate praise as one of the foremost hotels in the West. The grand opening, on the heels of a national scandal over Tabor's divorce from his first wife, Augusta, and remarriage to Baby Doe, kept Leadville's name in the headlines. The remoteness and isolation of the highest valley of the Arkansas had not kept Leadville from developing as other cities only dreamed of; there were gaslights, telephones, railroads, even one of the first electric generating units in Colorado. And as the smelters worked overtime casting 100-pound bars of silver and lead, industrialization was visible in another way — in clouds of noxious, poisonous sulfur and metal fumes and smoke that drifted over the city while tons of metal-based chemical wastes were dumped into the Arkansas River.

The miner, his ways, his attitudes, and his customs forged in the crucible of circumstance that were the Leadville mines, developed traits and practices that remain a part of his profession today. First, the miner was basically a transient worker. He was a transient when he came to the mines, and the nature of his job assured he would remain one. The miner, more than anyone, was poignantly aware of the imbalance that existed between his wage and his contributed effort and assumed risk. That imbalance alone dispelled any illusion of company loyalty, and the conditions in which he worked made the point absolute. Most miners hired on at a particular mine because of rumors, then left for the same reason. Most fully believed their mine was the worst in existence, and the rumors of employment elsewhere were received as a matter of the grass being greener elsewhere. In Leadville, a miner could work at any of a hundred mines, and justification to quit his present job was easily found; an unreasonable foreman, a bad accident, the departure of a trusted partner, tales of a better mine "over the hill," rumors of a mineral strike in another camp, or even a breakfast that didn't settle right. Any experienced miner could hire on elsewhere in a matter of hours, no questions

1889. Miners from the Louisville Mine, Leadville, about to begin another shift underground. Note the fresh candles and the "pie tins." Pie tins were the lunch bucket of the era, drawing the name from the meat pies that were the customary lunch of the Cornishmen. The name is still in use among miners today.

Colorado Mountain History Collection—Lake County Public Library

asked. Nor did supervisors have to worry about an inexperienced man masquerading as a hardrock miner. A single hour in the underground separated the miners from the imposters seeking a miner's wage.

This much-practiced freedom or "tramping," was an effective release for the tensions and frustrations of the job. The supervisor knew how many miners would work a shift only when they showed up, and not a moment before. It was said that a mine needed eight miners to handle the work of two in the underground, since two would be coming, two would be going, two would be out "rustling," or seeking work elsewhere, while two might actually be working on the job. When Leadville boomed, it triggered one of the greatest tramps in Colorado history, attracting miners from Georgetown, South Park, the San Juans, and every other camp. After a firsthand look at Leadville, many turned right around and were back at their old jobs a week later. Leadville was also a temporary seasonal home for many miners who saw nothing wrong with working during the summer months, then tramping for the silver camps of Arizona before winter set in. And if the warm climate of Arizona was too far, Colorado had many working hardrock camps thousands of feet lower and considerably more comfortable.

When the Cornish miners began their immigration from Britain in the 1830s to work in the midwestern lead mines, they brought with them skills, techniques, and customs that were quickly assimilated into American hardrock mining. Continuing their westward drift, the Cornishmen were present at the development of Nevada's Comstock Lode in the 1860s. When Leadville boomed, the Cornish contributions to mining included square-set timbering, headframe design, a type of steam pump used to dewater most mines, and, most importantly, a logical, orderly pattern of drilling, blasting, and mucking. Cornishmen also brought an economic scheme that made the hardrock miner as close to being a capitalist himself as he ever would be. This was contract mining, an arrangement in which the miner was paid not for his time, but rather for his output. This concept could work both ways, making it appealing to the miner and mine owner alike. The mine owner saw a grand opportunity to receive far more labor for only a slight increase in paid-out wages. The miner saw a grand opportunity to greatly increase his earnings by employing every trick to save time, effort, and material he could dream up.

Prior to 1882, Leadville's mine owners had no interest whatever in contracting, since the high profits that came from bonanza ore made labor costs insignificant. But when owners turned to lower grade ore, they were forced back to underground areas that had been improperly worked in the first place. These included caving stopes, workings with rotted or insufficient timber, or lower workings that may have been flooded. It was here, the mine owners agreed, that contract mining might very well have its place.

Teams of miners began submitting bids on certain underground projects, such as ore extraction or drift development. If accepted by the company, the miners began work, totally aware that their speed and efficiency would determine their profit or loss. Whatever the particular project was, it was sure to be a challenge, for mine owners issued contracts only on the more dangerous or difficult jobs. The mine owner hoped that, if there should be a loss, it would fall to the miners. Only the most accomplished and expert miner could consider contracting, and he would select only men of similar skills for his team. The material costs could be significant since they included timber, powder, fuse, and caps, and were the responsibility of the miner. Because of the amount of money involved, contract mining quickly developed into a game of wits. To the Cornishmen, it was considered the ultimate sport, a concept that spread rapidly throughout the mining West.

The contract miner's greatest resource was his expertise and ingenuity. Unfortunately, in his fervor to outdo the mine owner at his own game, he sometimes employed too many technical and economic shortcuts. Since both material and time were money, he blasted with insufficient powder, foolishly drilled and loaded powder simultaneously, and installed the least amount of timber he thought would do the job. In the process, he greatly increased his own personal risk of death or injury, frequently ruining the underground workings for those who would follow him. Cheating was accepted as part of the rules; ploys like cutting and retaping a supervisor's tape measure to his own advantage were an honorable and often profitable part of the game. As the number of contracts increased, so did death and injury rates for, unfortunately, each step that increased safety decreased production and footage. More than a few contract miners were carried from the mine in baskets after trying one shortcut too many.

Leasing was a variation of contract mining in which groups of miners leased mines or, more often, sections of mines. Leasing be-

70

came common in Leadville in the late 1880s when the increased costs of dewatering and working lower grade ores brought vanishing profits. Although many mines were now operating only on a break-even basis, owners hesitated to shut them down completely, leaving them open to the irreversible ravages of flooding. Mining teams who leased a section agreed to pay the owner a fixed percentage of the gross profit realized from the sale of ore to mills and smelters. Owners leased only those sections where they thought mediocre ore would be found, hoping to make a modest income while keeping the mine dry, which was the responsibility of the leasing miners. The miner's aim was to maximize his profit through every possible cut in costs and time. From the options open to him, the miner selected a section of mine where logic, intuition, or possibly some knowledgeable advice indicated the presence of a reasonably high grade ore body. In the end, leasing proved a failure for almost everyone involved; only a few miners ever made expenses, and those owners who were successful in keeping their mines dewatered found timbering so poor that many sections could never be worked again. A few groups of miners, however, did stumble into pockets of bonanza ore and walked away with small fortunes, never again to face the prospect of mining for $3.00 per day. The leasing system was perpetuated by the hopes of duplicating the few successes.

Ideas of miners and mine owners clashed on every major point; what seemed good for the miner was not good for the owner, and vice versa. The foremost example was the time-honored practice of highgrading, the miner's tendency to pocket pieces of particularly rich ore or of metallic gold or silver. Highgrading originated on the western gold placers, but was difficult because the sluices were in full view of everyone. Laborers were warned that their jobs involved shoveling gravel and nothing more, and that the only hands permitted in the sluice riffles belonged to the claim owner or his trusted manager. Highgrading in the gold placers was considered theft by the owners, accepted as such by the working miners, and punishment was meted out without controversy in every gold camp in the West.

The arrival of the hardrock mining era brought new attitudes and conditions that greatly increased both the potential and moral justification of highgrading. First, neither the mine owner nor his managers spent one second more than they had to in the dark, dangerous underground, leaving the miner to work mainly on his own. Secondly, the miner resented the wage-profit imbalance and the grave

71

risks he assumed; the miserable conditions of the underground generated no company loyalty. Highgrading, as one might expect, reached its peak in the hardrock gold mines. Throughout the frontier era, one ounce of gold — $20.00 — was the size of a small marble. To the miner, it represented a long week of drudgery in the underground. Refractory ores played no part in highgrading; it was the visible native gold that often ended up in the miner's pocket or lunchpail. To mine owners, highgrading remained a clear case of outright theft. To the miner, it was an earned right, paid in full with risk of his life and limb. Legally, the mine owners were correct. Morally, however, many sided with the miner.

The first hardrock mine in the highest valley of the Arkansas River, the Printer Boy, was doubtlessly well highgraded. Its ore included remarkable specimens of native gold in white quartz that drew acclaim on a nationwide exhibition. During its operational history, the mine produced about $750,000, or 37,000 ounces of gold, much of which was mined as what would today be referred to as "collector's specimens." Consider the plight of an early hand-steel miner returning to the muckpile to peer down through the drifting smoke at a week's, or even a month's, wage in the form of one small piece of gold-laden quartz. What was an honest hardrock miner to do?

Highgrading thrived even though mine owners took every security measure to prevent it. But the miner had ten long hours of dark isolation to dream up ways around the security. He succeeded admirably, demonstrating great resourcefulness and imagination, and holding no bodily orifice sacred. If caught in the act, the miner faced a charge of theft to which he pleaded innocent and stood a jury trial. His plea of innocence was based not on principle, but on knowledge that the jury would be packed with his partners, any one of whom might be in the same predicament next week. Miners were a tight brotherhood, quite capable of defending their "right" to highgrading.

The miner was well aware of what constituted worthwhile highgrade. Many Leadville district lead-silver ores were characterized by large, cubic crystals of galena, or lead sulfide, the size of which decreased proportionately as silver values increased. Very heavy ore with a matrix of fine, uniform, gleaming crystals was really silver-lead ore in order of values present. Much of Leadville's ore was locally distinctive, that is, it could often be traced back to the mine of origin. For a highgrader, that would never do. Nor could the highgraded silver ore be spent freely as a medium of exchange, since its exact silver content and value was uncertain. It was here that Leadville's legion of assayers entered the highgrading picture. Each assayer's office was equipped with a small charcoal furnace to reduce ore to its metal components — in other words, to metallic silver. The participation of assayers in highgrading schemes was also considered illegal but, since they, too, stood to make a profit, many worked a regular night shift behind locked doors busily smelting down highgrade. Owners attempted to stem the illegal practice by sacking the best ore right at the muckpile in the underground. The total value of highgraded ore was insignificant in comparison to the district production, but it made a big difference to the Leadville hardrock miner.

In the 1880s, the heart of the Leadville mining district was Fryer, Iron, Breece, and Carbonate hills immediately east of the city. Most mines were served with vertical shafts, the remainder employed horizontal or declined tunnels for access to the workings, and a few were open pits. The operations were of two basic types: small independent mines with a single shaft; and consolidateds, large, multi-shaft operations that exploited groups of claims in complex underground systems.

The smallest mines were similar to those of old Oro City. Lack of financial backing usually limited operations to hand steels and horse-drawn whims, with giant powder being the only affordable modern mining tool. Ventilation was poor and improved only if a second shaft was sunk for cross circulation. A fire could then be built at the base of one shaft, thus creating a draw at the other. If rich ore was struck, the mine owner rarely planned to mine it, but simply sold the mine at a good profit or entered into a consolidation.

The backbone of the Leadville mining district was the large consolidated operation supervised by the best mining men available. Solid financial backing assured the benefit of the latest mining tools. By late 1879, Fryer Hill was worked by nine consolidateds including the Chrysolite and Little Pittsburg which contributed mightily to Leadville's overall production. Those nine mines were served by thirty-one shafts. The total extent of workings is not known, but the Chrysolite alone had over a mile and a half of drifts. Carbonate Hill's three consolidateds were served by eighteen shafts, while nearby Breece Hill had thirteen major mines working through twenty-nine shafts. The geological variance in the ore deposits, together with vagaries of engineering design, assured there would be no "standard" underground configuration for the Leadville mines. Their only common feature was a relatively shallow depth. The workings at Nevada's Comstock Lode reached 3,500 feet to create unusually severe problems with water, heat, and ventilation. Leadville's ore extended from the surface to a maximum depth of several hundred feet, and a 500-foot shaft was considered deep. A look at a few of the major Leadville mines shows the variation in size, configuration, and production:

The **Robert E. Lee**, on Fryer Hill, which boasted the highest grade ore in the district, developed slowly through a single shaft as miners first encountered only low grade ore and water problems. After eight months of work, they blasted into a vertical vein of high grade mineral up to two feet thick. Within four months, the shaft reached 275 feet in depth and four lateral levels followed the bonanza ore. Miners exposed this bonanza vein for 115 feet, extracting ore containing from 250 to 500 ounces of silver per ton. The best ore was truly spectacular, although it was not representative of the overall vein. It averaged eighty-seven *percent* silver or about 20,000 ounces per ton. The Robert E. Lee never needed a consolidation and continued work through its single shaft. In nine days at the end of August, 1879, the mine produced $250,000, and a two-week period in October accounted for $115,000 more. In early 1880, a larger crew of 150 miners sank three additional shafts to exploit the large 100-ounce-per-ton ore body that surrounded the bonanza vein. That "low grade" ore had been left in place until the original vein was mined out.

The **Chrysolite**, also on Fryer Hill, was a large consolidated exploiting eleven claims over thirty-six acres. In 1880 it was the district's largest mine with a work force of 534 men, half working in each of two underground shifts. Among the nine shafts was the Roberts Shaft, the pride of the district. The 13x5-foot, 117-foot-deep shaft was divided into three compartments: two cageways, and a pump and ladderway. A seventy horsepower steam engine provided power and the Roberts was equipped with cages, timber guides, and the best wire rope available. Of the eight remaining shafts, four were powered by steam and four by horse drawn whims. 7,000 feet of workings exploited several 100x25x25-foot ore bodies averaging forty percent lead and fifty ounces of silver per ton. The best ore

74

specimens were native silver (horn silver) worth $10 per pound and doubtlessly well highgraded. In 1879, the Chrysolite's production costs were $10.65 per ton; by the end of that year, the mine had sold 60,000 tons at a profit of $60 per ton. Final development would take five more years and seven miles of drifts.

The **Breece Mine** was at first a 200-foot-wide and 15-foot-deep open pit exploiting a shallow, high grade iron deposit, selling the ore as a convenient flux to the Leadville smelters. After the mine changed hands in 1879, the new owners drove a shallow, declined drift through the pit floor to determine the limits of their ore body. At a depth of 35 feet, the decline was still rich in iron; a series of lateral drifts were developed which met smelter demands during the winter of 1879-80 and also provided a sheltered working place for the miners who had found the open pit work of the previous Leadville winter an ordeal. The Breece miners then drove through sixteen more feet of good iron, then into a layer of quartzite and porphyry that seemed to end the ore body. To confirm this, they drove the decline a few feet further — only to strike rich lead carbonate with increasing silver values.

Like other Leadville mines, ore transportation at the Breece was a small industry itself. Sixteen teams made two trips daily over the rutted three-mile road to Leadville, each wagon loaded with three and one-half tons of ore bound for the gaping, fiery maws of the smelters.

It was mines like these and a hundred others operating simultaneously that accounted for the total 1879 Leadville mineral production of $10,000,000. The Leadville *Herald* calculated that the silver produced that year amounted to 294 tons, or 7,000,000 ounces, that could be spun into a one-eighth-inch-diameter wire 1,980 miles long — enough to reach from Leadville to New York City. That silver had come from ore extracted mainly during mine development, and the great blocks of ore left in place seemed to assure substantial production for an indefinite future, an idea soon to change. That year also accounted for 9,000 tons of lead worth another million dollars. Iron mining contributed still more, as did gold which was still being mined in California Gulch and more frequently encountered in the ores of several hardrock mines.

Since there was no central mine agency, such as a bureau of mines, there are no accurate records of the extent of the underground workings. Such data was kept only in supervisors' work books or on engineers' drawings, and only for the larger and better organized mines. The numerous smaller mines had no need for such records; they opened by the hundreds and, if no ore was struck, or if water flooded the workings, closed by the hundreds. Closing a mine, in the 1880s, meant simple abandonment. The workings flooded and soon collapsed, burying with them the record of their extent. Still, based on a United States Bureau of Mines survey conducted decades later, Leadville's miners drove over 150 miles of underground workings during the silver boom years from 1878-1890.

TYPE OF WORKING	NUMBER	APPROXIMATE EXTENT
*Shafts	1,000	60,000 feet (11 miles)
*Prospect Holes	1,400	14,000 feet
Tunnels	125	18,000 feet
Total Underground Footage, including drifts, crosscuts, winzes, stopes, declined tunnels, etc.		800,000 feet (150 miles)

* (A shaft is considered a vertical working from the surface with a collar and supportive timbers; a prospect hole is a simple, unsupported vertical digging.)

The job of driving 150 miles through solid rock using the tools of the 1880s, at an elevation of over 10,000 feet, requires no accompanying words. It is clearly one of the more monumental of all frontier achievements. From the incredible effort expended to accomplish this feat came the silver and other metals that bought every board and brick that built the city of Leadville. And every foot of those 150 miles was in turn bought with sweat, human suffering, and human life. Leadville's miners, in the 1880s, were soldiers in a head-on conflict between their own human endurance and fallibility and the effects of the poorly understood and poorly controlled mechanical innovations of mining. Those miners employed every trick they knew to tear the silver from the rock, but magic was not one of them.

Through the 1880s, production was maintained by mining larger volumes of lower grade ores and the development of new mines. The "Downtown" mines were developed within the eastern limit of the community sprawl of Leadville with their headframes jutting up between houses. These shafts were considerably deeper than the earlier mines and also 500 feet lower in elevation which created worsening water problems. Still, the grade of ore was high enough to warrant expensive pumping operations. Enormous steam pumps were used with the tonnage of water pumped from most mines far exceeding that of the ore extracted. Several times miners drilled into subterranean water channels with near disastrous results. Although a catastrophe never occurred, miners sometimes narrowly escaped death in the black, rushing, icy waters. Several shafts were flooded nearly to their collars, requiring enormous expense to dewater.

As silver continued to pour from the Leadville mines — 5,000,000 ounces in 1890 — improvement in rock drills brought further weight reduction and greater operating efficiency. Drills that first ran on fifty pounds of air pressure were adapted to operate on eighty pounds; together with advances in steel cutting edge design, drilling was faster than ever. The accompanying cloud of rock dust was also thicker than ever.

By the mid-1880s, the most tragic sight in Leadville and the other mining camps was that of hundreds of terribly debilitated miners whose coughing and shortness of breath had weakened them beyond performance of their jobs. Mine owners "let them go" and others, younger and stronger, took their places beside the thundering drills. Since hardrock mining prepared a man only for more hardrock mining, these broken men faced a bleak future. Some owners, out of sorrow or guilt, offered them trivial jobs on the surface for $1.00 per day, usually cutting the wooden wedges which the underground crews used by the millions.

It was no longer questioned that "miners' consumption" was related to the inhalation of rock dust churned up by the drills. Although doctors had not yet arrived at the exact medical explanation, the term "rocked up" and "dusted" had become a permanent part of the miners' vocabulary. Also, the full potential of the disease — that it was frequently terminal — had become all too evident. Because of Leadville's elevation, her miners suffered more than those of lower camps and often developed serious complications. Through ignorance of the disease, it was considered shameful; neither miners nor mine owners discussed it openly. Accordingly, it will never be known how many miners became "rocked up" and died a slow, horrible death. Leadville funeral records show many men in their twenties and thirties dying of "consumption" and other pulmonary problems, but the true extent of the disease was not apparent, for many stricken miners departed to seek relief at lower elevations. Those who did not die within a few years carried the debilitation with them for the rest of their lives.

By 1890, medical researchers had positively identified the physiological causes of the disease. As most already suspected, it was the inhalation of rock dust created by dry drilling, mucking, crushing, and hauling in the underground. The silica dust was composed of finely pulverized bits of quartz, porphyry, and granite which, under microscopic enlargement, were shown to possess needle-sharp edges capable of scarring and destroying delicate lung tissues. The lungs were incapable of dissolving the tiny particles of rock which, in time, released silicic acid to literally petrify the elastic lung tissues. The result was a gradual reduction and, finally, elimination of the lungs' ability to provide the blood with oxygen. The afflicted miner simply smothered to death. The irreversible disease had no cure or relief, and its appalling death rate earned the mechanical rock drills the name of "widowmakers." The disease was formally named silicosis, but miners continued to use the terms "rocked up" and "dusted" for what had probably already affected them, too.

In the 1890s, several states passed laws forbidding the use of the widowmaker drills. Mine owners challenged the laws, bringing the matter to the United States Supreme Court which supported the prevailing attitudes of the era, ruling that if a man took employment in a hazardous industry, it was "tough luck" when the hazard caught up with him. Any legal or moral responsibility on the owner's part had been fulfilled with payment of the weekly wage. Furthermore, the Court stated that a company was in no way obligated to alleviate or eliminate the hazard if doing so would cost it money. The bottom line of the rulings assured the rich would become richer and the miners would continue to get rocked up in the underground.

Considerable thought had been given to elimination of the rock dust problem, and the answer seemed to lie in a hollow drill steel that could convey a stream of air or water. This concept, however, required rolled steel, still a technological impossibility. Holed steels could be manufactured using gunbarrel techniques, but only at prohibitive expense. The burden of overcoming the rock dust problem was finally assumed by a man who had witnessed the first Colorado trial of the Burleigh drill in 1870. J. George Leyner, the former hardrock miner and now engineer who had breathed his share of rock dust in the underground, procured some of the first rolled, drill-quality steel ever manufactured. In 1891, he designed a drill that forced a jet of compressed air down the hole in the steel to the cutting edges where it escaped in a rush, an arrangement very effective in clearing the hole of drill cuttings as soon they accumulated. Leyner manufactured seventy of these drills and sold them to Colorado hardrock mine owners. About half of those drills were shipped to Leadville and quickly lowered down the shafts. True to Leyner's word, the holes cleared as they were drilled, and the new efficiency made drilling faster than ever. The accompanying cloud of rock dust, however, became so thick that the miners could literally not breathe at all and refused to drill with the "Leyners." At the risk of personal financial ruin, Leyner took every single drill back and began redesigning. In 1893, he designed and fabricated another drill. This model utilized not air, but a column of water, no simple engineering feat. The result instantly and totally eliminated rock dust and even provided other beneficial effects including cooling of the drill steel, automatic flushing of drill cuttings from holes, and creation of a cutting mud which acted as a highly effective wet grinding compound to further speed up the drilling process. J. George Leyner had accomplished one of the premier breakthroughs in mining technology, one whose significance challenged the invention of the rock drill itself.

Unfortunately for the miners, the transition to wet drilling did not happen overnight. Mine owners had huge sums invested in the widowmakers, drills which could not be converted to Leyner's new water system, and had no intention of scrapping the old drills. Drill manufacturers all turned to the "wet" designs which the owners accepted even though their old drill steels were now obsolete. Their concern was still not for the health of their miners, but rather to benefit through the increased efficiency of wet drilling. Every state eventually passed anti-dry drilling laws, but the widowmakers, laws or not, continued in use well into the 1930s, especially in smaller mines.

Other advances in drilling included the first pneumatic extension "air leg" which mounted the drills on a universal joint. The first models were extremely dangerous because of the weight of the drill and poor control of extension of the leg. While engineers worked to perfect the air leg, most miners gladly went back to drilling "off the column." The 1890s also brought the first practical diamond core drills that enabled miners to sample subterranean strata much more cheaply than through driving exploratory shafts and workings. The new core drills found immediate use in Leadville and were responsible for the opening of several new mines and increased production from old ones.

In the mid-1880s, the rapid expansion of railroads provided new outlets for the skills of Leadville's hardrock miners. Aspen, twenty-five miles west across the Continental Divide, founded in a silver strike in 1880, was in full production by 1885. A connecting railroad project was begun to provide easy access for Aspen ores to the Leadville smelters. Plans called for a 2,060-foot-long tunnel passing beneath the Divide just north of Mt. Massive at an elevation of over 11,500 feet. Driven through solid granite, the tunnel would be ten feet wide, twelve feet high, and supported by massive redwood timbers. Many miners tramped the silver mines to become "railroad miners," starting the bore in 1886 and blasting through a year later. Railroad tunnel development was similar to drift development, but on a grander scale. The first trains ran through the Hagerman Tunnel beneath the Continental Divide in July, 1887.

Another railroad tunnel project was commenced in January, 1890, this one at Tennessee Pass, fifteen miles north of Leadville. Again, more Leadville miners received wages not from a mining company, but from a railroad, this time the Denver & Rio Grande. The project was a 2,600-foot tunnel to eliminate a steep, tortuous right-of-way and would also pass beneath the Continental Divide. The Denver & Rio Grande wasted no time, working not only from each end, but also from several shafts sunk into the middle. Leadville's miners completed the bore in only eight months.

Still another rail tunnel project, this one the biggest of them all, commenced driving virtually beneath the old Hagerman Tunnel in the summer of 1890. Built to reduce the costly snow removal problems that plagued the old Hagerman, the new bore would also accommodate the larger and heavier standard-gauge rail equipment just making its appearance. The Busk-Ivanhoe was 9,364 feet long and driving it was no easy job, taking three years and the lives of

80

more than twenty miners. When it was completed, comfortable, well-appointed trains rolled between Leadville and Aspen beneath the Divide, marking the beginning of a new era in mountain transportation. The three rail tunnel projects kept Leadville in the headlines, but nowhere was mentioned the fact that nearly forty more miners had been killed, twice that number maimed, and no one would ever know how many "rocked up."

After 1885, Leadville's silver production leveled at about 5,000,000 ounces annually, about half that of 1880. The price of the metal, however, had declined from $1.16 per fine Troy ounce, to $1.00 in 1890, with users unable to absorb the cumulative production of the western hardrock camps. In 1890, after a major political battle, the Sherman Silver Purchase Act was passed by Congress' obligating the government to support the price of silver by purchasing 4,500,000 ounces each month. Passage of the Act brought a sigh of relief to western silver interests, but the price continued to fall and, by 1892, stood at 87¢ per ounce. In 1893, western silver men were shocked when the Sherman Silver Purchase Act was repealed, allowing the price of silver to seek its own free market level as determined by supply and demand. As expected, the downward trend was accelerated. In 1890, Leadville's production had been based on 100 active mines; three years later, only twenty mines could economically continue to operate. The silver situation contributed substantially to the Panic of 1893 which closed many banks across the country. In Leadville, smelters also shut down as mines ceased operations. The miners, in a desperate effort to prolong their own employment, accepted a wage reduction of 50¢, lowering their daily wage to $2.50.

The miners, however, had a few options open, for the collapse of the silver market and subsequent closure of many silver mines happened to coincide closely with the last great precious metal strike in the continental United States. Only seventy miles away, on the slopes of the mountain that lent its name to the 1859 rush, lode gold had been discovered. Shafts were quickly sunk around the area of the "float" discovery to encounter some of the most remarkable gold ore ever found in the West. In 1893, *the* name in western mining was suddenly Cripple Creek; many of the Leadville miners facing unemployment packed their gear and tramped.

While the silver disaster of 1893 was permanently closing many lesser camps, Leadville managed a recovery. In spite of a depressed price hovering around 63¢ per ounce, Leadville's mines stepped up

81

production to 9,000,000 ounces, a total nearly matching the 1880 production. Much of the resurgence was due to the Little Jonny Mine, part of the Ibex Properties complex, which was now Leadville's leading gold and silver producer. More importantly for the long term, base metals such as copper and zinc were beginning to achieve economic prominence. In many Leadville mines, silver production was already secondary to that of base metals. It was now becoming evident that the future of Leadville would no longer ride on silver, but on the variety of metals in the district.

The major organizational developments in labor that had already affected other western mining camps finally reached Leadville in 1895. The Western Federation of Miners, the first miners' union of real strength, began to attract the Leadville miners. In June, 1896, the inevitable happened. Following the pattern of labor disturbances in other camps, Leadville erupted. Mine owners refused to meet wage increase demands, just as they had sixteen years earlier. The miners struck and the owners locked them out. Bitter miners, goaded by labor agitators, retaliated with violence, arson, and even murder until order was restored by the Colorado Militia. Martial law was imposed and owners brought in scab labor to work the larger mines under the protection of the guns of a small army. What little respect the miners had left for the owners was destroyed once and for all; the hatred that developed between them would endure to mar labor relations for many decades. The Leadville winter of 1896 was marked by repeated attempts of mine sabotage, but the presence of some 800 Colorado Militiamen kept the situation in control. The owners stood fast; by spring, 1897, the striking miners grudgingly accepted the fact that the combined power of the owners, politicians, and the State Militia could keep them locked out forever. On March 9, 1897, the miners broke and returned to work, ending a strike that lasted nearly nine months.

During the nine months of inactivity in many mines, shafts flooded, timbers rotted, inundated ground "swelled" to collapse workings, and the lowest levels were completely silted in. Although the strike was over, the devastation in the underground prevented rapid rehiring. In some cases, years were needed to bring mines back to operational status, and many never reopened at all. By 1898, the silver price had slipped further to 58¢ per ounce, mining slowed, layoffs were common, and the miners bitterly resented that their wages had never even been restored to their original $3.00 per day.

82

To make matters worse, Leadville was about the only district in Colorado that had not gone to an eight-hour shift in the underground. As the new century neared, the glitter had disappeared from both Leadville and the silver it mined. Even the legendary figures whose names were once synonymous with booming Leadville were no more. The greatest of those names, and the one that would live forever, was H. A. W. Tabor. Horace Tabor had played a remarkable role in frontier history; he had come west with the "Fifty-niners," labored in the gravels of California Gulch with a gold pan, then rode the silver boom to unimagined heights. His own story had paralleled that of Leadville; the town had gone from a collection of cabins to the most glamorous mining camp in the West; Tabor had gone from a placer miner and storekeeper to a millionaire and to high political offices in Denver and Washington. And now that the glory of Leadville had faded, so had the glory of Horace Tabor. When the silver market collapsed, so did Tabor's investments. And as Leadville, the once glamorous Silver Queen of Colorado fell on hard times, H. A. W. Tabor, once the greatest silver baron of them all, died in poverty in Denver in 1899. Both the fact and circumstances of his passing were symbolic of the end of the silver era.

As Tabor was buried in Denver, the smelters continued to cast their pall over Leadville while producing increasing amounts of the base metals, reflecting the trend of western mining in general. A severe winter with heavy snowfall closed out the 1890s, bringing to an end the rampant expansion and development that characterized the frontier. It had been a monumental nation-shaping adventure; now, almost gratefully, it was history. The blanket of snow that covered the highest valley of the Arkansas River also covered deep, permanent scars gouged by four decades of hell-for-leather mining. Where there had been nothing but wilderness, the gravels of California Gulch had given birth to tiny Oro City; that, in turn, had been swallowed by the excitement of Leadville, a city whose own wild, brief youth was gone before it ever knew it was young. Beneath the snow lay a tired, old city awaiting the coming of spring and the fortunes, if any, of a new century.

The valley, once remote and isolated, was now connected to the world by telegraph and telephone wires, and by railroads from three directions. Its niche in history was assured, but only at enormous cost. Forests had been reduced to fields of stubble, and the cut timber lay rotting in the flooded darkness of the underground. Hillsides were scarred with yellow dumps of waste rock that guarded a thousand forgotten shafts, portals, and prospect holes. Still active mines, reached by rutted, muddy tracks, stood among mines that would produce no more. The great hills of Fryer, Iron, and Carbonate still yielded their mineral treasures, but lay covered with abandoned headframes and hoist shacks, their timbers slowly weathering alongside piles of drill steels, pipe, cable, rail, and spikes, all slowly rusting away to nothing. Leadville was a dreary city of brown and gray hidden beneath the white of winter snows, a city overbuilt in the furor of the silver rush, and now a hollow city of empty cabins and houses beginning their long, slow period of decay. Outside the still-smoking smelters, enormous heaps of black, man-made slag drained their acid metal wastes into the weary Arkansas. And along Harrison Avenue where silver barons once proudly walked, stooped men, weak and aged beyond their years, bundled themselves against the winter winds and coughed.

The Leadville miners had fought and suffered through a great technological revolution of mining. But who had won? It might be said the miners won, for they had torn from the rock, with old and new tools, over $250,000,000, mostly in gold and silver. The miners never benefited from this fortune; in fact, they paid dearly for the privilege of mining those ores. In the Leadville district alone, in the twenty years that followed the great silver strikes, 400 miners died in accidents and more than 1,000 were maimed. Many more coughed themselves to death with dusted lungs, or were enmeshed in that slow, inevitable process. The tragic story of the Leadville miners was repeated throughout the mining West from the Coeur d'Alene mines of Idaho to the mines of Bisbee, Arizona on the Mexican border. The collective human cost of mining the western frontier's mineral treasures exceeded 7,500 miners killed and 20,000 more maimed, a macabre toll to which the mines of Leadville readily contributed their share.

Six thousand *tons* of Leadville silver assured the city a prominent place in history books. And the historians wrote the story as they felt people would prefer to read it: as an exciting fantasy of magical wealth. And so it was that Leadville's image was one of gamblers and whorehouses, grand hotels and silver barons, and not of the mines and miners who made it all possible.

It was a rare miner who could write lasting words. But Lazar Jurich, a first-generation European immigrant, was one. From his

Leadville, Colorado, 1888, looking west across the highest valley of the Arkansas River toward Mt. Massive and the Continental Divide through the smoke of the smelters. The base of California Gulch, its gravels thoroughly worked, may be seen at left.   Lake County Civic Center Association own experience, he sang the sad song that told of the miner in his ballad "Underground in America."

> For the mine is a tragic house,
> It is the worst of prisons —
> In bitter stone excavated,
> In barren depths located —
> Where there is no free breath,
> By you always burns a lamp,
> And your body struggles with the stone.
> Hands work, never do they stop,
> And your chest sorrowfully heaves,
> For it is full of poisoned smoke,
> From gelatin's powder white.
> We, miners, sons of sorrowing mothers,
> Look like men from the wastelands.
> In our faces is no blood
> As there is in other youth.
> Many poor souls their dark days shorten,
> Many poor souls with their heads do pay.
> There is no priest or holy man
> To chant the final rights.

In the coming new century, the Leadville miner was ready for a better lot in life. He had earned it on the mining frontier.

PART III

The Molybdenum Miners

In 1900, Charles Senter was nearing sixty, still living quietly in his simple cabin near Fremont Pass, which had already long been known as Climax, named for the site of a station house at the top of the long uphill grade of the Denver & South Park Railroad. The old prospector, who had experienced much of the frontier in both time and deed, continued to work the Ten Mile gravels, washing out just enough gold to pay for his few needs. He still did a bit of hardrock prospecting, in the fading hope of making the gold strike that had eluded him twenty years earlier. He also steadfastly performed the required annual assessment work on his Bartlett Mountain claims. And in the corners of his cabin still lay the dusty canvas bags containing the mineral samples he had collected from Bartlett's barren, rocky slopes. The white rock with the black streaks was no longer the mystery it had been when Senter first discovered it back in 1879, for European chemists had finally identified the mineral as a sulfide of molybdenum.

Fremont Pass before the development of the molybdenum deposits. Bartlett Mountain is shown at the left and the Pass looks much as it did when Charles Senter discovered his "graphite."   Climax Molybdenum Company

Molybdenum, the metal, had first been identified as an element in 1778 by the Swedish chemist Carl Scheele. Its name was derived from the Greek *molybdos*, meaning "lead-like," a fitting description of the pure metal. Molybdenum existed as a laboratory curiosity for well over a century with no known practical use. About the time Senter learned of the true nature of his "gold" claims on Bartlett Mountain, the French were developing the first applications of the metal, aware that small percentages of molybdenum alloyed with steel significantly enhanced the toughness of armor plate.

In 1901, chemists at the Colorado School of Mines in Golden, Colorado, confirmed the Bartlett mineral to be molybdenite, the only important source of molybdenum in the world. As local interest in the deposits grew, other prospectors arrived at Bartlett Mountain. Hugh Leal, in 1905, staked claims near Senter's; several years later, Leal and his miners, without benefit of a rock drill, performed extensive hardrock exploration work. Single jacking and blasting their way 400 feet into the side of the mountain, Leal's miners encountered nothing but molybdenite the entire distance. As knowledge and in-

88

terest in molybdenum grew, other prospectors and speculators arrived to stake claims. Even though molybdenite was no longer a mystery, what to do with it was; no market existed for the metal, nor had a suitable recovery process been devised.

The early 1900s, for many once-proud western mining camps, were years of severe economic depression. In 1902, the many mines that had somehow survived the 1893 collapse now shut down. Only the highest grade silver ore, of which there was very little left, could be mined profitably. To worsen the situation, lead, nearly always associated with silver ores, had dropped to only 3ᶜ per pound. Those camps with no other metal ore resource — and there were many "silver only" camps in the Rockies — finally gave up the ghost, or perhaps took in the ghost, as the case may be, for these years marked the birth of many true western ghost towns. Their mines were closed, allowed to flood, and finally to collapse. People left, never to return, leaving only a few old-timers to keep an eye on the ghosts and the memories, and perhaps to await a revival that would never come, at least not through mining.

Leadville still was not destined for such a fate, thanks to its complex and diversified mineralization. But times were hard after the silver collapse in 1893; Leadville, too, was depressed and bore little resemblance to the boom city of 1880, yet the emergence of base metals assured its survival. The most important were copper and zinc which came into full production in the early 1900s. Also helping was a resurgence of gold production, most of which came from the Ibex Properties. In 1905, Leadville's total mine production was $11,000,000 from five metals. Gold accounted for 10% of production, copper for 6%, lead and silver for 22% each, and zinc, now the leading district money maker, accounting for 40%. Iron and manganese made up a fractional part of the total value, and provided a convenient and economical flux for the smelters.

The highest valley of the Arkansas River, which once produced only gold, then virtually all silver, now had a relatively balanced production of metals. The industrial demand for base metals reflected both advanced metals technology and a greatly expanded and broadened American manufacturing capability. Wooden wagons had yielded to steel cars and trucks. Railroads expanded and the growing electric power industry consumed more and more copper. Leadville no longer relied on a single metal, boom town economy, but enjoyed a

89

new economic stability and diversity. The economic base, of course, remained mining, but the diversity lay within the mining. Both Leadville and its miners began to benefit directly from the metals they produced. A city-wide electrical system was put into use in 1901 and improving rail service had stabilized prices at levels only slightly higher than those of Denver.

In 1905, 3,000 Leadville miners extracted 650,000 tons of ore. Their predecessors of 1880, 4,000 strong, had mined only 140,000 tons. Twenty-five years of advances in mining had increased the production capacity of an individual miner by five times. Nothing as remarkable as drills or giant powder had appeared, but steady improvement in tools and techniques not only increased the miner's production, but also his standards of health, safety, and general welfare.

Explosives had been widely improved. Dynamites became available in many grades and strengths, enabling miners to better control the size of the fractured rock in their muckpiles. Most significant was the addition of chemical antifreeze compounds to all dynamites to lower the freezing point of nitroglycerin, thus ending the dangerous separation problems. The introduction of the electric blasting cap, with its positive, safe detonation, brought a further reduction of accident rates in the underground. Electric caps improved rapidly, first through desensitizing the fulminate of mercury, then with increased manufacturing quality control, and finally with the perfection of the "delay" electric cap, permitting miners to precisely time the detonation of various charges within a shot.

Carbide lamps, first used on English bicycles, were introduced to mining in 1892 and by 1900 had replaced candlelight in the underground. The lamp was a two-part device, the top part containing water which dripped at a regulated pace into a quantity of calcium carbide in the lower unit. A chemical reaction produced acetylene gas which was directed through a nozzle mounted in the center of a concave reflector. Ignition produced a spit of flame which, aided by the reflector, was far brighter than any candle. The lamps were difficult to extinguish accidentally, a big advantage over the candles which could be snuffed out in the act of lighting a fuse, leaving the miner in total darkness holding a "hot" fuse. Miners had previously used headbands to hold candles to their hats, but since the traditional soft hat did not hold the heavier lamp well, the first protective headgear, a peaked rawhide hat, was introduced. The rawhide dried

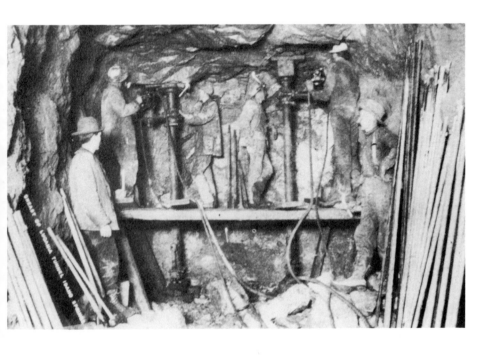

Hardrock drilling after the turn of the century. The drills shown are the newer type utilizing J. George Leyner's "wet" drilling concept, as confirmed by two hoses leading to each drill, one for compressed air, and the other for water that eliminated the rock dust hazard. Note the numbers of steels of various lengths that will be dulled in the course of drilling this one face. Note, also, that while the drills are of the most "modern" design, the light is still from candles.

Colorado Historical Society

91

after being shaped into a hat, becoming quite hard; for its weight, it was the next best thing to metal. Lamps were clipped onto slots sewn into the hats. The brighter, more reliable carbide lamps brought yet another reduction in accident rates underground.

Drills became lighter, more powerful and more reliable, thanks to advanced steel alloys that made both more durable drill components and harder, longer-lasting steel cutting edges. Denver had become a major manufacturing center for all types of hardrock equipment. The companies that would eventually merge into Ingersoll-Rand and Gardner-Denver, names familiar to every working miner today, were already well established. J. George Leyner continued his work on the rock drill, forming his own company which was eventually acquired by Ingersoll-Rand. Leyner himself, the old hand-steel miner-turned-engineer who did so much to benefit his fellow miners, was killed in 1927, not the victim of a mining invention, but of another, the automobile. Today, Leyner's name appears in heavy, embossed, steel letters on many of the most popular models of the modern rock drill.

The most revolutionary advancement in mining in the early 1900s was the arrival of electricity. Electrical power was first used in mine haulage in 1882 in Saxony, England. Four years later, it was attempted unsuccessfully in a Pennsylvania coal mine. In 1899, the first practical electric haulage system was installed in a West Virginia coal mine. As early as 1908, eastern coal mines were experimenting with electric drills using auger bits on soft coal seams. The few attempts to adapt electric drills to hardrock use were absolute failures. Although the electric drill would be of little hardrock use, there was no doubt that electric power, particularly in haulage and hoisting, would be a big part of future underground mining.

Electricity came to the Leadville district in 1906, with the completion of the Yak Tunnel and the Yak power plant. The tunnel was two miles long, providing drainage-haulage service to many mines. When the power plant went on-line, the tunnel was electrified and the first of the legions of Leadville mules were retired. Only months later, tall steel towers carrying 100,000-volt power transmission lines leapfrogged over the mountains which, twenty-five years earlier, were breached only by treacherous wagon roads. The Colorado Power Company, with two large hydropower plants in the state and a steam auxiliary plant in Leadville, was quick to realize the potential of the hardrock mining industry as a customer. Leadville received its power from either of the two hydro plants, using its own substation to step it down to a useable 6,000 volts. The steam plant was rarely used, but was kept on standby for the benefit of the mines should the main power source fail. By 1908, ninety percent of Leadville mines were using electrical power. Especially for smaller mines, steam power became uneconomical. Electric mine equipment such as winches and locomotives were available for one-quarter the cost of a steam system generating the same useable power. As copper wires jumped from mine to mine, hundreds of boilers and miles of steam pipes were torn out and left to rust.

Electric fans finally brought truly effective ventilation to the underground. The huge steam pumps used for dewatering were scrapped, and replacing them were specially designed centrifugal pumps powered by 550-volt motors that easily pumped 1,500 gallons of water per minute from an 800-foot-deep shaft. Steam hoisting equipment was also hauled to the junkyards as smooth, reliable electric winches now raised and lowered the shaft cages. Mining embraced electricity so quickly there was no time to iron out the many operational problems. In the early 1900s, very few men were aware of the dangers of electricity in normal industry, much less in underground applications. Some of the early voltages employed were enormous for what was actually necessary. That, coupled with poorly insulated cables in the wet workings, inevitably produced fatal accidents. Although electricity would find wide use in mining, its early years brought tragedies reminiscent of the first dynamites and the early drills.

The innovations in drills, explosives, power, and lighting were not employed in every mine; although the technology was now available, it would be many years before the mining industry would be truly modernized. Since modernization was a matter of economics determined by the mine owner, the largest mines changed quickly, while many small mines had to continue using mules and hand steels. Although the widowmaker drills were no longer manufactured, they were still used by the thousands and would be until they literally wore themselves out. In hardrock mining new ways came hard, and old ways died harder still.

Along with technical advances came new and enlightened social concepts. In the early 1900s, the Leadville miner still earned $3.00 per day, but, at last, his shift had been reduced to eight hours. The importance of and concern for the hardrock miner was being realized.

Drilling contests among the best miners were major events all over the mining West. This photo taken at the turn of the century shows the large crowd that turned out on Leadville's Harrison Avenue to watch (and bet on) the single-jacking and double-jacking miners who competed for large cash prizes.

Colorado Mountain History Collection—
Lake County Public Library

High grade ore mined by lucky prospectors was history; lesser ores efficiently mined by experienced men would be the future of mining. Underground death and injury rates, although still unacceptable by today's standards, were only a fraction of those in 1880. Most larger mines now provided injury insurance for working miners, and a few had taken the remarkable step of offering compensatory payment to widows upon the deaths of their miner husbands.

Hardrock mines had always been free of regulation; supervisors were responsible to owners; owners, possibly, to a major financial backer. The owner's word, always directed toward greater production, was absolute law. The first hint of the possibility of state regulation came in 1889 when Colorado passed an Act creating an "Inspector of Metalliferous Mines." This position was created with the clear knowledge that the "Inspector" would have no real power. In these years, the power of Colorado's mine owners made it politically im-

94

prudent to attempt regulation of their activities. Inspectors would be tolerated as long as they did nothing to interfere with production. Accordingly, the Inspector of Metalliferous Mines busied himself collecting mineral specimens and documenting production. This position was abolished in 1895 when another Act established the Colorado Bureau of Mines, headed by a Commissioner. The Commissioner of Mines was charged with, among other things, "the supervision of metal mine inspection and the enforcement of laws relating to health and safety in metal mines." There were few mining laws on the books to enforce, and a politically wise Commissioner who liked his job antagonized no one. Still, the Colorado Bureau of Mines, in its early years, did make some constructive contributions to the safety of the working miner. The first positive action was standardization of the shaft bell signal code. Underground accidents that once went unrecorded were now tabulated by cause and location in a manner that would point out areas and operations of unusual danger. Mines with notoriously poor safety records became subject to closer scrutiny with the threat of enforcement always becoming stronger. In 1908, fifty-five fatalities were recorded among Colorado's 20,000 hardrock miners. Thirty years earlier, the Leadville district alone would have accounted for that number of deaths. Three decades had brought an eighty percent reduction in death and injury rates and with each passing year, additional laws were passed, many directly connected with the health and safety of the working miner.

In 1913, Congress created the United States Bureau of Mines to document mining activity and enforce new federal mining regulations. Both state and federal mine bureaus were backed by authority and political approval, and pressure was finally brought to bear on mine owners. Hardrock mining was still dangerous, but mines were no longer underground factories that simply used human life to produce ore.

Another change in mining was the continued decline of the small company. The future of western hardrock mining was already in corporate hands which developed further the mass mining of enormous tonnages of low grade ores. Success demanded the largest and most advanced mining equipment available, and most of it was priced beyond the resources of a small company. In 1860, an individual miner on his own claim was in a better position than the "company" miner who worked for a fixed daily wage. Now the situation was reversed; it was the corporate miner who worked more safely and with better equipment, and who was beginning to enjoy significant social benefits.

By 1910, Leadville was a functional mining town. The population had leveled at 7,000, almost all miners or those working in supporting industries. No longer did the wanderers come to Leadville for excitement and adventure; if they came at all, they came to work in the mines. Leadville had already embarked on a lonely course apart from the mainstream of national development, where cities would enjoy growth and continual renewal. Leadville would remain stagnant, now bound to the fortunes of hardrock mining. But the source of the fortune was changing; although district mines still produced, the future lay twelve miles away at a railroad whistle stop called Climax.

Ex-Sergeant Charles Senter, the old Indian scout, quietly celebrated his seventieth birthday in 1912; thirty-three alpine summers had passed since he staked his claims on Bartlett Mountain. This was the year he was to meet Otis Archie King, a young mining manager-promoter-scout who, as jack-of-all-mining-trades, represented a mid-west banker seeking mining investment opportunities. King was among the first to express serious interest in the molybdenum claims, purchasing the options from Senter for $40,000, payable as $500 down and $50 per month against the purchase price. Over the next few years, King helped design a flotation-separation process in a Leadville mill that was effective on a number of ores, including the first molybdenite ever mined commercially from Bartlett Mountain. The milling and separation process yielded about two tons of molybdenum sulfide concentrate which King sold to a metal alloy company in the East. At the time, 1915, it was the largest quantity of molybdenum sulfide ever shipped, and enough to meet world demand for two years.

Meanwhile, Germany geared up for war with armaments recognized as the finest in existence, thanks in large part to their new molybdenum-steel alloys that were vastly superior in hardness and durability. Molybdenum was still rare, and the Germans acquired their entire supply from a single mine in Norway that exploited a molybdenite deposit occurring in veins only a few inches thick.

When the outbreak of World War I provided positive proof of the superiority of molybdenum-steel alloys, the interest of industry and mining turned suddenly to Bartlett Mountain. A confused flurry of

96

claims, lawsuits, counter claims, and backroom financial maneuvering followed — all aimed at gaining control of what was already recognized as the world's largest deposit of molybdenite. Three corporate interests dominated the battle. From the beginning, the leader was the American Metals Company, the United States corporate arm of the German corporation *Metalgesellschaft*, which owned forty-nine percent of Amco's stock. Amco established the Climax Molybdenum Company in 1916 to investigate the Bartlett Mountain deposit. With Max Schott, their Denver representative, spearheading the Colorado venture, the Climax Molybdenum Company picked up the options on other Bartlett claims. Also in the battle were the Molybdenum Products Company and Otis Archie King's group. The bleak mountain pass at 11,318 feet elevation, previously the site of only the Climax station house, now had small crushers and mills, several trestle-like aerial tramways to convey ore from the mine portals, and bunkhouses and facilities for a work force of 300 men. Many of the first Climax miners and millhands were Spanish-Americans and Mexicans, part of the first major migration of that ethnic group to the Leadville region, a movement spurred by the availability of work at Climax and the border disturbances created by the Mexican Revolution.

A government-ordered reorganization of the American Metals Company brought divestiture of the German interest but did not hinder the Climax Molybdenum Company from winning the battle for Bartlett Mountain. Its strong financial position overpowered the other hopeful developers. In 1918, Otis Archie King sold his group's interest to the Climax Molybdenum Company for $300,000. Although King had lost the battle for control, his group, thanks to his own valiant efforts, managed a respectable profit. Perhaps more importantly, King in later years would write *Gray Gold*, a colorful book telling the inside story of the early development years of the Climax mine.

And what of Charles Senter? When King sold out to the Climax Molybdenum Company in 1918, Senter finally received the bulk of his $40,000 option. Payment had been a long time in coming, for Charles Senter had staked his first claims on the windy, rocky slopes of Bartlett Mountain thirty-nine years earlier, at a time when Leadville was booming and other men searched for silver. When his claims had finally been sold, Senter left the mountains, moving to Denver where he spent his remaining years with his foster daughter. He left

Early development on Bartlett Mountain in World War I. The site is above timberline and subject to a harsh alpine climate.

Climax Molybdenum Company

no legacy of opera houses and grand hotels, but his life had touched the Civil War, the Indian Wars, and the heyday of the frontier. History would forget his name, but his discovery of the white rock with the black streaks on Bartlett Mountain would indeed have its memorial. Not many years after Charles Senter died on February 12, 1924, his original Bartlett claims would be developed into one of the greatest mines in the world.

The World War I mining activity on Bartlett Mountain was brief, for the end of hostilities in Europe killed the demand for molybdenum. The stockpiled "moly" could meet and surpass foreseeable world demand, and the Climax operation shut down in March, 1919. The loneliness of the Fremont Pass winter was again broken only by passing trains as alpine winds whipped through tramway timbers already falling into disrepair. Some wondered whether the young Bartlett Mountain mine was already bound for the graveyard of forgotten shafts.

The year 1920 was dismal not only for Climax, but also for Leadville, twelve miles "down the hill," then deep in the throes of a post-war metal price depression. The industrial mobilization that created demand for molybdenum also increased demand for base metals, and in 1915 and 1916 the prices of copper, zinc, and lead reached their highest levels in many years. The Leadville mines had hired all comers and increased production, shipping huge tonnages of ore to smelters working around the clock. In 1916, the district produced $2,100,000 in gold, $1,900,000 in silver, $500,000 in copper, $1,500,000 in lead, and a whopping $10,000,000 in zinc. The total district production was over $16,000,000 which, in current dollar value, topped even the best years of the silver boom. Even miners shared in the increased profits, receiving $4.00 for an eight-hour shift underground. With the war over, metal prices plummeted to rock bottom in only two years, and Leadville again tottered on the brink of disaster. The district's entire 1921 production was only $1,750,000, one-tenth that of 1916.

Businesses and mines closed, miners were laid off, and the fortunate few who stayed on accepted another 50¢ per day pay reduction. The population dropped to 4,500, most of them unemployed. In such times, Leadville could be a very depressing place, and the economic woes were compounded by another round of serious health problems. In 1919, a national influenza epidemic swept into the city taking 200

99

lives. The brief rise of molybdenum was shadowed by a wartime base metal boom, but it hardly mattered in 1921. The base metal markets were glutted, and molybdenum had no market at all. Gold and silver, Leadville's old glory metals, were no longer viable economic bases. After six decades of mining and a staggering total metal production of $400,000,000, the highest of any single mining district in the United States, Leadville seemed ready to join her sister mining camps in oblivion. Though it was a small consolation, Leadville could rest assured that her history and enormous metal output would make the city a ghost town that time would never forget.

Yet while metal prices would remain depressed for the next decade, Leadville was still not through. The city and district clung tenaciously to survival on the production of a handful of active mines, and work was being done to sell the peacetime potential of molybdenum to American industry. The American Metals Company had launched its own research and development program to create a market for molybdenum by devising practical applications and uses for the metal. Brainard Phillipson, one of the company's young metals men, was assigned to lead the effort. He accomplished his task quickly and capably, convincing engineers and designers that the extraordinary qualities of moly steel were suited for far more than tank armor and artillery barrels. Leading Phillipson's list of potential moly steel consumers was the rapidly expanding automobile manufacturing industry. Automotive engineers, along with those of other industries, became aware of the benefits of high-stress moly steel alloys. So Brainard Phillipson succeeded in creating a market. By 1924, the wartime stockpile of molybdenum was exhausted and the Climax Molybdenum Company, with sole control of the mining interests on Bartlett Mountain, resumed operations.

The Climax mining operation would be a totally new concept, different from any mining ever conducted in Leadville or in the West. Molybdenite was present in two huge superimposed ore bodies, unlike deposits ever mined before. The grade of ore was also new; historically, Leadville's ore had averaged $20 per ton. When Otis Archie King made the first commercial sale of molybdenum sulfide concentrate, he received $35 for a twenty-pound unit. Since he had recovered only one pound of concentrate from every ton of ore, that made each ton as mined worth only $1.70, a figure earlier Leadville miners would have ridiculed. To compound the seemingly illogical economic aspect of molybdenum mining was an inefficient milling and separation process with its poor recovery percentages. Many Leadville mines closed because their remaining reserves were "only" five times more valuable than the Climax ore. The only favorable factor seemed to be the sheer quantity of ore within Bartlett Mountain. To make this grand plan profitable, ore would have to be mined and milled on a scale never before considered. Modern hardrock mining was about to begin.

In 1924, the Climax Molybdenum Company had most of the necessary mining tools to begin a massive mining program on Bartlett Mountain. Wartime research had benefited mining technology immensely. Explosives were more powerful and safer than ever, and new alloys made drills and steels more durable. Drills now operated on 100 pounds of air pressure while the improved steel cutting edges battered through ten feet of rock before reforming and resharpening became necessary. Most importantly, it was electric power that enabled Climax to take on the job of mining molybdenite.

Although carbide lamps still served the individual miner, electric light bulbs now lit the underground. The fragrant mules that had pulled a millon ore cars could hardly begin the job Climax had in mind, and in their place came the "electric mules," beasts of infinite and untiring power. This new mechanical breed of mule took nourishment not from a feed bag, but from a 400-volt trolley line. It dropped no offal on the drifts, for its gut was nothing but a massive direct current electric motor born to haul ore cars. And haul it did. Only a few years after resuming operations, Climax was using electric locomotives weighing over twenty tons each that pulled underground ore trains laden with 200 tons of ore.

A block cave system of mining was planned. The first step was extensive core drilling to determine the shape and grade of the ore bodies within the mountain. Then a pattern of large haulage drifts was constructed beneath the ore body. The individual 10x12-foot drifts were usually supported by twelve-inch square timber sets, although in places the drifts advanced "baldheaded," that is, relying upon the inherent stability of the rock itself. The floor of each drift was laid with heavy, thirty-six-inch-wide rail, strung overhead with 400-volt trolley line. Along the side, or "rib," of the drifts, miners mounted three pipes; two carrying compressed air and water in, the other conveying drainage water out. Drift development followed a time-honored pattern of drilling, blasting, mucking and timbering. When blasted, the four-foot rounds produced a twenty-ton muckpile.

Miners now mucked from rail-mounted pneumatic mucking machines that tossed hundreds of pounds of rock at a bite into waiting ore cars. Electric locomotives effortlessly trammed strings of loaded ore cars to the portal. And when a drift was completed, it became part of an extensive underground railroad system designed for continuous, efficient ore haulage.

Immediately above and perpendicular to the haulage drifts, smaller drifts about 100 feet long were constructed, each connected to the haulage drift below by a drawhole at its center. These were called "slusher drifts," and each was equipped with a powerful pneumatic winch to operate a cable-rigged drag bucket. From each slusher drift, a pattern of still smaller workings, called "finger dashes," was driven upward into the ore body. From these, long holes were drilled upward deep into the solid ore. When loaded and blasted, large sections of the ore body were fractured. Now broken and loose, the shattered ore fell by gravity through the finger dashes into the slusher drifts. From there, the ore was mechanically dragged by cable buckets to the drawhole where it again fell by gravity into ore cars positioned below in the haulage drift. Entire trains could be quickly loaded through coordinated signals between the train motorman and the slusher operator.

Cave block development was slow and expensive, but, upon completion, could move huge tonnages of ore with the work of relatively few miners. The system was highly energy-efficient; at no point within the mine was it necessary to raise the ore vertically. All movement was accomplished by gravity except short horizontal travel in the slusher drifts and haulage drifts where trains rumbled day and night.

In the early years at Climax, development was combined with production of just enough ore to meet the still-limited demand for molybdenum. That demand soon increased as a result of the American Metals Company research and development program, an aggressive advertising campaign, and the successful sales efforts of Brainard Phillipson. The giants of American industry, including Ford Motor Company and the Timkin Roller Bearing Company, began specifying molybdenum-steel alloys from their suppliers. And, of course, there was one place in the world for the steel producers to obtain molybdenum. In 1929, the Climax Molybdenum Company recorded its first profit. For many years, that profit would be reinvested into further development of the mine and mill and the research program to keep abreast of the competition from other alloys.

A major obstacle to development was the location; both the mine and mill were located at timberline, 11,300 feet above sea level. Those who thought Leadville was cursed with a bitter winter had only to see Climax to change their minds; on many winter days Leadville would seem a comparative garden spot. Snow fell every month of the year at Climax with an average annual fall of about 300 inches. Temperature could frequently fall to twenty below zero and lower. But the surface conditions posed no problem for the underground. Away from the portals, the temperature stabilized at about forty degrees with only slight seasonal variation. The miner, however, could not live in the underground, although that may have been better than the pitifully inadequate surface bunkhouses. Most miners lived in Leadville, and on many winter days it was a job in itself to reach the mine to start the shift.

The eight-hour shift, even with the new mechanical tools that moved more rock faster, remained a physical challenge. Drills battered the miner's eardrums and, even with improved ventilation, every blast still released smoke, dust, and gases that ended up in his lungs. Sometimes, if water was not available in a particular working, the miner would drill "dry," just to "get the job done." Rock dust was also stirred up from the new mechanical tools, especially the slusher buckets, mucking machines, and ore trains. All underground mining equipment took such a terrible beating it had to be constructed in the heaviest manner possible. Everything the miner touched during his shift took a substantial effort to lift. Drills weighed 160 pounds, timbers and slusher buckets weighed a half-ton each, and heavy rails and ties were moved and spiked by hand. And in the many areas that the mechanical muckers could not reach, the shovel could.

Development at Climax was accompanied by injury and death, but at rates that continued to decrease. Although underground work was generally safer, the miner now faced snapping cables, the elastic backlash of which could decapitate him, high-voltage electric shock, the hazard of falling rock, and the crushing type of injury common around heavy mechanized equipment. Lurching pneumatic mucking machines, the miner found, seemed to spend more time off rails than on, and derailing in a single, violent second could pin him between steel and rock. In the haulage drifts, derailing of the heavy muck train could kill a miner before he even knew he was in danger. Once derailed, the heavy motors and cars required a hazardous, grueling effort with jacks and timbers to get back on the rails. The thin air of the extreme elevation made matters worse. The miner, even though accustomed to underground work, could experience dizziness, nausea, shortness of breath, or extreme fatigue that might last the entire shift.

Discontented miners were common in any mine, but stepping from the underground after a rough shift into the bitter alpine winter could make any miner complain. Increasing numbers of Climax miners confronted their supervisors and, in their inimitable prose, voiced their complaints, collected their pay, and tramped. Others quickly replaced them but they, too, became disillusioned and joined the ranks of the departing. After only a few years of operation, the Climax Molybdenum Company faced one of the highest turnover rates in all of American industry. Climax was already the largest mining operation Leadville had ever seen and its need for steady labor grew daily. On some days, the peak of activity took place not in the mine or mill, but in the Climax personnel office where long lines of miners simultaneously went about the business of hiring on and tramping. Even forty years later, a few would-be Climax miners accomplished both feats in a single shift.

Company management decided to alleviate the labor turnover problem with a company town. The company town concept was nothing new to western mining, having first been tried in the 1890s in the copper camps of the Southwest. When Climax began planning their town in 1928, the company town image was already badly tarnished. Names like Bingham, Utah and Bisbee and Jerome, Arizona brought visions of row after row of dreary clapboard houses constructed of timber scraps and old powder boxes salvaged from the mines. The company towns were places where employees bought from the company store, banked at the company bank, worked in the company mine or mill, and generally had their personal decisions made by the company. Some believed the entire system was carefully structured to insure that a worker never achieved financial independence that might bring personal freedom and mobility. As the muckraking journalists pointed out, the product was a company slave, a worker upon whom the company could always rely. There was certainly some truth in this, for no company town ever threatened to become a utopian community. Conversely, neither were the independent mining towns that were built by individuals with all the personal freedom they could muster. A good example was Leadville; in the 1920s, the city was a random collection of structures, both occupied and abandoned, built of everything imaginable and lining streets and ruts that wound through slag heaps, headframes, and piles of debris left from a half-century of a "live for today and to hell with tomorrow" philosophy. Climax never had any real social motivation to construct its company town; the company simply provided facilities to induce miners to stay, at least for the start of the next shift.

While the Climax Molybdenum Company worked at its problems on Fremont Pass and laid the foundation for what would become the largest underground mine in the country, Leadville faced its own problems. Metal prices remained depressed and mine production in the old district was lethargic. Several dewatering projects were funded in hopes of stimulating production. The Canterbury Tunnel was begun in 1921 to dewater mines on Fryer Hill and parts of Iron and Carbonate hills. Eight years and 4,000 feet later, after the tunnel failed to encounter any commercial-grade ores, the project was abandoned. A more successful project was started in 1923 using enormous steam pumps to dewater several previously important producers. The dewatered mines were leased and began sporadic production in 1925.

Gold, and for a while, lead, were the only metals to maintain price levels through the 1920s. Lead production meant risking hardrock expenses, which few owners were willing to do in those uncertain years. Gold, which remained fixed at $20.67 per ounce, got renewed attention throughout the highest valley of the Arkansas River, on both individual and corporate levels. Long forgotten, rusted gold pans were taken from sheds and old boards hammered together to make sluices. Although every gold bearing stream in the valley had been worked, a skilled and patient miner could still wash yellow metal from the gravels. A man would no longer strike his fortune, but with employment hard to find, an ounce of placer gold looked inviting. Through the 1920s, a miner and his partner swinging shovels alongside a wooden sluice once again became a common sight near Leadville. With a lot of hard work and a little luck, a living wage could still be found in the sluice riffles.

It was a corporate interest in gold that brought one of the more notable placer operations to the highest valley of the Arkansas. Beginning in late 1913 and continuing for two years, a steady stream of prefabricated steel components rolled west over the railroads from Yonkers, New York, on the Hudson River, to the upper Arkansas River. Near Lake Creek, the shipments were offloaded and sorted out. For nine months, a small army of welders and mechanics assembled the steel puzzle. In the summer of 1915, 600 tons of timber, steel, cables, buckets, and electric motors was ready. The "mountain boat" had arrived in the Leadville district.

The mechanical gold dredge originated in the New Zealand gold fields in the 1880s and spread quickly to the American West where large volumes of low grade gravels remained. Such gravels could be worked profitably only in a volume operation like that of the electrically-powered mechanical gold dredge. In 1915, the Derry Ranch Gold Company dredge, constructed, owned, and operated by the New York Engineering Company, represented the latest in gold dredge design. On October 10, 1915, operations commenced with the mechanical grating and clanking of steel buckets, the sounds of yet another form of western mining.

The Derry dredge had a 120-foot-long floating wooden hull, an overall length of nearly 300 feet, and was basically a huge specialized sluice box. At the front of the dredge was a long boom suspended by cables from a large, overhead steel frame. On the boom was mounted a continuous dragline of twenty-eight, six-foot-wide steel buckets. In operation, the bucket dragline gouged its way into the river gravels, scooping five cubic yards in each bucket, and conveying it to the interior of the dredge where hoppers separated and sorted the gravels, the finest of which were directed to a long metal sluice at the rear. The tailings — virtually all the material the dredge ingested — were carried out the rear on seventy-five-foot-long conveyor chutes and dumped in heaps. The dredge moved an enormous amount of gravel and consumed a similar amount of power, receiving 13,000 volts from the Colorado Power Company. Its own transformer stepped this down to 2,200 volts to power the four main digging and pump motors. A further stepdown to 440 volts provided power for a variety of secondary pumps and devices.

The Derry dredge first worked the broad gravel shelves near the mouth of Lake Creek on a 1,200-acre leased group of claims. The bucket line could dig to a depth of thirty feet, creating a deep cavity while imparting a slow forward motion to the dredge itself. Stream diversion or pumping water into the huge hole formed a lake in which the dredge hull floated. The lake would "move" with the dredge as the

The Derry Dredge, built by the New York Engineering Company, and shipped piecemeal by rail to the highest valley of the Arkansas. In this photo, the dredge is owned and operated by the Mt. Elbert Gold Dredging Company of Leadville and shown in operation in Box Creek about 1925. The "footprints" of the dredge are just as they were left – as endless piles of boulders still very much in evidence today.

Colorado Mountain History Collection—Lake County Public Library

bucket line dug out a cavity in front, then filled it in behind. The environmental effect of the dredge was disastrous; only a few months of work could actually render topographical maps obsolete. Streams were diverted, ponds created, and banks destroyed as the creaking, clanking dredge devoured everything in its path. Stream pollution was monitored by the Colorado Bureau of Mines but was not a problem; if operated properly, the dredge's lake acted as a settling pond for the tons of silt that were stirred up. And behind it, the dredge left its "footprints": thousands of neat, conical, well-washed heaps of river boulders, nearly all of which may still be seen today.

The dredge crew of twenty-five men had little to do with mining in the conventional sense; their efforts were directed toward continual maintenance necessary to keep the dredge operating. Both the buckets and their sleeve bearings were made of the hardest manganese steel available, but since they operated immersed in quartz sand, their effective lives were very short. Most of the miners' time was spent lubricating with heavy greases and replacing bearings. From time to time, an enormous boulder would jam the bucket line, shear pins would break, and the dredge would grind to a halt. Every effort was made to free the bucket line with bars and levers. If that failed, the boulder would be "pasted," that is, blasted with a small quantity of dynamite "pasted" on its surface. Great care would be exercised, of course, to prevent the ultimate ignominy, that of blowing part of the dredge to pieces. If pasting failed, a rock drill was kept on hand for the ultimate solution.

The winter brought icing conditions that made operations impossible. A steam boiler was first installed. When that failed, a large electric hot air furnace followed. Results were apparently satisfactory, for the dredge, its clanking and grating now accompanied by great clouds of escaping steam, dug its way through the next four winters.

The Derry dredge operated at a profit for its first four years. In only two months after it had been assembled, the dredge washed 150,000 tons of gravel to recover $69,550 in placer gold, or about 3,500 ounces, a ratio of about one million pounds of gravel to every pound of gold. That was the highest grade gravel the dredge would ever work. As operations progressed, the gold-bearing gravels became erratic, but the dredge still earned a profit as it worked its way onto the banks of the Arkansas River. The New York Engineering Company saw that its dredge received great publicity in the East, noting it to be "one of the most successful dredging operations ever conceived."

By 1920, the Derry claims at the mouth of Lake Creek were a barren desert of rock piles with all the suspected commercial grade gravels worked out. Operations were suspended during 1922 and 1923, a period the New York Engineering Company wisely used to sell the dredge to the Mt. Elbert Gold Dredging Company, a newly formed Leadville company with hopes of repeating the successful operation on their own claims. The dredge was disassembled and shipped five miles north along the Arkansas River to Box Creek, ten miles south of Leadville. The dredge clanked to life again in July, 1924. It operated sporadically, tearing up the alluvial flats well, but never recovering its 8¢ per cubic yard operating cost. The clanking stopped forever on September 25, 1926; the dredge was disassembled again and shipped to Central America where richer gravels awaited its attention. The mountain boat was gone, but never to be forgotten, for in its wake were thousands of acres of ugly rock piles, its contribution to the mining heritage of the highest valley of the Arkansas River.

The following year, the miners' limitless ingenuity found another way to coax a bit more gold out of the Arkansas gravels. Near Granite, where the first prospectors had panned in 1859, operations were begun by the International Hydraulic Dredge Company, a group not nearly as imposing as its name. Working from a beamy wooden barge thirty-eight feet long, International used suction dredges for the first time ever on the Arkansas. Two diesel engines powered pumps that literally sucked the gravels from the river bed and dumped it into sluices. In its brief two-year period, International did very well. In its best runs, a crew of only four men worked 400 cubic yards of gravel per day. Expenses, after purchasing equipment, were minimal, and the gravel averaged a value of $2.00 per yard. In the late 1920s, few men in Leadville made a better living.

In 1930, the Climax Molybdenum Company, still in its infancy, was also doing well. As the sole United States source of molybdenum, the mine now accounted for five percent of Colorado's annual metal production. Leadville was hit hard by the depression and the $3,200,000 molybdenum production of 1932 was the only encouraging statistic. That year, the Leadville district, excluding Climax, listed only twenty operating mines, fourteen working part time, and ten with no production at all. The production of only 4,300 tons of ore forced the closing of the smelters. Leadville's population dropped to its lowest ever at 3,400, as did the price of silver, to only 28¢ per ounce. Base metals offered no help, for copper had dropped to 6¢ per pound, and both lead and zinc to 3¢ per pound. In 1932, the Leadville district mines accounted for a total mineral value of only $143,000, far below the $16,000,000 of 1916. Gold accounted for ninety percent of production.

Gold mining was dramatically stimulated as the nation began its recovery from the depression. The end of the gold standard and devaluation of the dollar hiked the value of one Troy ounce of gold to $35. Leadville's gold production tripled within three years, with hardrock production substantially supplemented by placers. It is difficult, if not impossible, to document placer gold production. Hardrock production is accurately recorded through milling, smelting, and refining operations, but it is very unlikely that Leadville's placer miners marched to the newly-established Internal Revenue Service office to honestly report their production. Leadville's *documented* gold production rose to $600,000 annually, a level that would be maintained into the 1950s. Gold was not the only metal that came to Leadville's rescue; silver and the base metals made good recoveries and, by 1937, the district once again achieved the million dollar level in production.

On Fremont Pass, the 1930s proved to be a decade of great expansion and the Climax Molybdenum Company was rapidly becoming a wonder of the mining and industrial worlds. The otherwise conservative 1939 Colorado Bureau of Mines Annual Report referred to Climax as "famous" and "colossal." The development atop Fremont Pass would have defied the imaginations of the 1880s silver barons, and certainly made old ex-Sergeant Charles Senter smile in his grave.

A broader spectrum of American and world industry joined the steel mills that clamored for more molybdenum. Moly was now used in a variety of alloy steels, stainless steels, cast irons, and the first generation of "exotic" alloys. Other manufacturers began finding use for molybdenum compounds in paints, lubricants, agricultural fertilizers, and an endless array of chemicals. Expanding steadily to meet the growing demand while benefiting through solid management and brilliant engineering, Climax was building a mine and mill second to none. The 1880s silver boom became insignificant before the Climax production figures. In 1939, Climax employed more than

110

IVE GOT A PURDY GOOD HOLD OF
ER-GUESS I'M READY TO GO NOW, $6.15 A DAY
AINT BAD-BEATS FARMIN' ALL TO HELL.
CLIMAX

*A picture postcard showing a Climax miner in the late 1920s or early 1930s.
Work was hard to find in these years and Climax was one place where it could
be found. The caption is self-explanatory. The drill in this photo is still "dry."
Note the carbide lamp that has replaced the candle.*
Colorado Mountain History Collection—Lake County Public Library

111

1,000 men, half working in the cavernous underground beneath Bartlett Mountain. That year, molybdenum production amounted to $17,000,000, one quarter of the total metal production of the State of Colorado. Eighteen million pounds of moly concentrate had been milled from 5,000,000 tons of molybdenite ore. To achieve that production, Climax had mined 15,000 tons of ore every day.

A few comparisons may aid in appreciating those figures. In 1932, the entire Leadville production had been 4,300 tons for the entire year; Climax now tripled that in a single day. In 1880, at the peak of the silver boom, annual ore production was 140,000 tons, and now Climax surpassed that total every eleven days. The individual miner's production in 1880 varied greatly, but was probably less than two tons every ten- or twelve-hour shift. The Climax miner now mined twenty-five tons per eight-hour shift. The human cost of mining had changed perhaps the most of all; in 1880, fifty miners were killed and more than 100 maimed in the course of mining their 140,000 tons of ore; in 1939, only two Climax miners died in the mining of 5,000,000 tons of ore. In 1940, the Climax Molybdenum Company received one of the highest overall safety awards in the State of Colorado, earned on a man-hour basis in comparison not only with other major mines, but with general heavy industry as well.

Underground mining, by its nature, would always be hazardous. Fifteen Colorado hardrock miners died in accidents in 1939, one of the lowest fatality records since the State Bureau of Mines began keeping those statistics back in 1895. The great reduction in fatality rates was achieved while mining an infinitely greater tonnage of ore and rock. These statistics reflected the continuously improving conditions in the mines, but did little to console the grieving family of the miner hauled out dead.

In 1938, the Climax company town was ten years old and included 175 fully occupied modern homes of four to nine rooms each. Climax now had a United States Post Office, the highest in the nation (like most everything else at Climax), and facilities for dancing, movies, entertainment, and sports such as skiing and basketball. There was even a small gymnasium for general physical conditioning, if the miner didn't get enough exercise in the underground. Labor turnover rates were still high, but the success of the town had changed many of the "here today, gone tomorrow" attitudes of the first Climax miners. Climax always attracted new men, in hopes of making miners out of them, through regular recruitment programs, especially in the Mid-

112

Another picture postcard showing the "joys" of taking "five" in a powder magazine in the Climax underground about 1930. Climax was already well on its way to becoming the largest mine in Colorado and the United States.
Colorado Mountain History Collection—Lake County Public Library

west. Many young men found Climax an ideal place to pick up a "grubstake" for other adventures. The cost of living in the company town was modest, meals were generous, and lunches were even available for a miner to take underground. There were some things the town could not provide, however. Among them were suitable outlets to answer the call of the wild among the young miners. Leadville catered readily to these callings with a lengthy string of bars and, although now illegal, some gaming tables and a few whorehouses. An enduring relationship was established; Climax provided the wages and Leadville, the aging Silver Queen, provided the places to spend them.

A broader regional economic dependence on Climax was also developing. The highest railroad in the country, a spur of the Colorado & Southern, was converted to standard gauge and freight trains now crept daily along a breathtaking right-of-way to the always-expanding Climax mine and mill. And as highways and automobile travel improved, Climax miners could live further away and still report for their shifts on time. The full economic impact of Climax would be shadowed a bit longer, for another World War was imminent and the base metal mines in the old Leadville district were again gearing up for production.

Increased demand in the late 1930s had pushed prices of silver, copper, zinc, and lead to historic highs. In 1939, the Leadville district had forty-nine active mines, a number to soon double with wartime production. Leadville's smelters fired up again and thousands of tons of critically needed metals were recovered not only from newly mined ores, but also from the district's numerous mine dumps and slag heaps. Advanced separation and recovery processes, together with the economic incentive afforded by rapidly rising metal prices, turned acres of waste into commercial "ore." Molybdenum had been declared a strategic metal and the Climax mine and mill were ordered to full capacity to meet the burgeoning demand. Leadville contributed very significantly to the war effort, and in an oddly balanced way. Climax produced the molybdenum to make the finest gun barrels in the world, and the Leadville district produced, among other things, lead: 11,000,000 pounds of it in 1943, much of which was eventually sent through the moly steel gun barrels in Europe and the Pacific. Mention was made of this in the Colorado Bureau of Mines 1943 Review of Mining Districts. After describing active mines and ores, the report concluded with:

114

This economic surge in metals and mining peaked in the early 1950s, carried along on the postwar boom and the continuing demands of the Korean War. The last great years for the old Leadville district were 1951 and 1952 with an annual production of $6,000,000. In 1952 the Leadville mines poured out 18,405 ounces of gold, 322,000 ounces of silver (at a high 90¢ per ounce), 325,000 pounds of copper, 12,000,000 pounds of lead, and 17,000,000 pounds of zinc. But the following years brought a sharp decline in production of all these metals, caused by increased mining costs and wartime depletion of the few remaining higher grade ore deposits. Although commercial grade ore remained, economic factors had effectively shut down, at least for the time being, one of the most productive and historic mining districts in the West.

But the city of Leadville still was not about to become a ghost town, thanks to the Climax Molybdenum Company, which achieved new production highs with each passing year. Advances in milling increased recovery efficiency, not only for molybdenum, but also for tin, tungsten, and iron pyrite (iron sulfide), co-products of the separation process. Climax now produced 9,125,000 tons of ore at a value of $22,000,000 annually, one-third of the metal production of the entire state of Colorado.

One of the last attempts to prolong the life of the old district was the Leadville Mine Drainage Tunnel, begun in 1943 under supervision of the U.S. Bureau of Mines. An underground tunnel was driven from the Arkansas River just north of Leadville south to the Downtown mines where core drilling had indicated appreciable commercial grade ore reserves. Leadville mines drilled and blasted their way "baldheaded" through competent rock, advancing the drift 1,023 feet in a single month in 1944. The rapid development halted in 1945 when the federal appropriation was exhausted and a reduced peacetime metal demand made renewal of the project politically unattractive. But when metal demand picked up in 1950, the project was resumed. Work was finally terminated in February, 1952, after the tunnel had advanced over 12,000 feet and tied into the collapsed workings of several Downtown mines. Technically, the tunnel was a success, draining 4,000 gallons of water per minute. Practically, however, it was a failure, draining only abandoned, collapsed mines

115

and dumping the water, acidic and high in dissolved metal content, into the Arkansas River.

Even gold, which had given Leadville its start back in 1860 and carried the city through thick and thin, had its last good year in 1952. Eighteen thousand ounces were produced then, mostly from a large dragline operation working the same gravels in Box Creek where the mountain boat had sailed forty years earlier.

A very limited production of silver and base metals was still recorded in the Leadville district through 1960. This came not from mine production, but from slag and dump processing along with smelter cleanup preparatory to the final shutdown of the furnaces. In spring, 1961, the last of the smelters that had operated for eighty-three years was dismantled and scrapped. The noxious smoke that was a symbol of mineral prosperity for Leadville faded forever.

At Fremont Pass, however, Climax continued its expansion based on growing domestic and international demand. Molybdenum was now the only metal the United States produced in sufficient quantity to export. And as the fortunes of moly rose, so did the fortunes of Leadville. When Climax stumbled a bit, Leadville knew it. A strike in 1958 was followed by a longer strike in 1962. The degree of economic dependence on Climax became clear to all as Leadville slumped into its own local depression. It took six months for the union and management to reach agreement; when they did, 2,000 miners and millhands returned to the job, Climax paychecks were again issued regularly, and the Leadville economy recovered almost overnight. When the old district shut down, a few residents thought Leadville would do well to develop a second economic base, one free from the ups and downs of mining. But the regularity of the Climax paychecks tempered any action in that direction. By 1960, Leadville had become dependent not only on one metal, but also on a single producing mine.

Phasing out the Climax company town began in 1960 when additional space was required for expansion of the mill. Over ten years, Climax closed the town facilities in an orderly shutdown; miners and millhands moved to Leadville to take up residence there or in surrounding towns. Many of the original town buildings were also moved intact to Leadville where they assumed new functions as houses, stores, and apartments. Remaining at Climax was an enormous mine and mill, a U.S. Post Office, a misleading town dot on highway maps, and memories of what had been the highest town in the United

116

States. The Climax town would never be mentioned along with those whose names suggested manipulation and supression. When the company store finally closed its doors, the opinion among those who had been associated with the town over its forty-year history ranked it among the very best.

Hardrock mining had now become a very specialized industry, growing harder and harder for the general public to understand with every technological advance it made. The metal hardhat, a long overdue safety feature, made its appearance in the 1930s. By the end of World War II, the familiar carbide lamp had been replaced by electric, and now most miners wore rechargeable batteries on their belts with cords leading to bright electric cap lamps. Safety made another step forward when ear and eye protective devices came into use in the 1950s.

Drills, smaller and more powerful than ever, weighed one-third that of the original machines and were manufactured of super alloys finally capable of withstanding the severe stresses of hard rock drilling. The detachable drill bit, with carbide steel cutting edge inserts, brought an end to the piles of dulled steels awaiting resharpening and reforming. More and more drilling was performed by hydraulic drill rigs mounted on rail or rubber tire carriages. Typical was the "Jumbo" which mounted two rock drills on movable booms that provided a ten-foot drill advance without changing steels. The miner now operated the Jumbo fifteen feet removed from the face and beneath protective timber, drilling out a round of fifty two-inch-diameter, ten-foot-deep holes in one hour. The perfection of pneumatic extension "air legs" made obsolete the clumsy steel columns that supported the drills for seventy years. In their place stood a single skilled miner with a "Jackleg" drill and a few steels, able to "punch" a six-foot-deep hole anywhere in the drift in less than five minutes.

Mining advanced also in administrative and conceptual areas. Both the state and federal Bureaus of Mines, which earlier were mere compilation, advisory, and promotion offices, now had broad enforcement authority together with the political backing to use it. Regular mine inspections now assured compliance, or at least the effort to comply, with growing lists of underground health and safety regulations. Inspectors were vested with the power to shut a mine down on the spot, although prudence and common sense greatly tempered this authority. A constructive compromise between mine

117

Climax miners about 1950 posing for photo in front of the Phillipson Level portal. The Phillipson served as the main Climax production level for nearly four decades. Note the preponderance of safety warning signs. The industry was already becoming very safety oriented.

Climax Molybdenum Company

118

bureaus and companies was established, and the myriad of health and safety regulations became part of underground life.

Another reduction in underground accident rates came with safety education. No longer were inexperienced men hired off the street, given some gear, sent down the shaft, and left to learn the hard way. Orientation for "new hires" and regular safety meetings for working miners were now part of the job. Safety became a major company expense, supported for three good reasons. First, the value of the experienced miner was higher than ever — considering the increasingly sophisticated equipment he used, his loss was a company liability. Secondly, a higher accident rate brought greater attention from inspectors, possible fines, and other administrative actions. Finally, moral justification itself had evolved; the labor attitudes that characterized the American industrial revolution and the early days of hardrock mining had become outdated in the face of enlightened social values. In 1966, of a total of 5,200 underground miners in Colorado, only four were killed. The twentieth century had reached the underground.

Compliance costs for safety and environmental regulations could be borne only by large corporations; the era of the independent miner, and even the small mining company, was through. Even as late as the 1960s, a few two- or three-man groups with a single drill and a hand-trammed ore car attempted mine development, either to follow a vein of high grade mineral, or, more likely, to bring about the sale of proven property to a larger company. They were subjected to every single safety regulation that applied to the corporations. Money was often not available to put into "nonproductive" compliance, or even to fake compliance, and most small mines closed.

In 1966, Climax employed 2,100 people and was the largest employer in central Colorado. Production that year was $91,000,000, with five percent coming from the co-products of tin, tungsten, and iron pyrite. Molybdenum recovery set another record: 56,000,000 pounds of moly sulfide concentrate extracted from 14,000,000 tons of ore. The Climax Molybdenum Company was now mining 42,000 tons of ore every day.

While Climax was making history, the old Leadville district had passed into it. The 1966 recorded production was so low — eight ounces of gold, two ounces of silver, and no lead, zinc, or copper at all — that the Colorado Bureau of Mines stopped keeping production figures. Over a 106-year production history that began in 1860, the

119

The Climax Molybdenum Company operation at Fremont Pass in the late 1950s. The formation of the glory hole on the side of Bartlett Mountain has become quite prominent and was caused by mining millions of tons of ore underground. Many of the buildings in the photograph are part of the Climax company town which was about to be phased out because of growing mill space requirements. Climax Molybdenum Company historic Leadville mining district, excluding any Climax production, had produced over $500,000,000 in gold, silver, lead, zinc, copper, iron, and manganese using every form of mining ever employed in the American West.

Back in 1879, the Leadville *Herald* boasted of Leadville's immortality as a mining town, basing that optimistic projection on what they then thought to be inexhaustible reserves of silver ore. The prophecy, generally, was correct. The town was immortal; the metal was not inexhaustible. Leadville did indeed survive to the present without compromising on a mining history and heritage second to none in the United States. All the mines, all the metals, and all the miners played their individual parts in this wonderful, yet sometimes tragic, history. And in the end, the final burden was borne almost solely by what represented the epitome of modern mining science and technology, that colossus atop Fremont Pass, the Climax Molybdenum Company.

PART IV

The Present

Like thousands of others, I came to Leadville for the Climax Molybdenum Company. It was a matter of needing a job and, as usual, Climax had plenty to offer. Within a day I had hired on as an apprentice miner and moved into the Vendome Hotel, nee Tabor Grand Hotel, the same once lavish and widely acclaimed hostelry built by H. A. W. Tabor during the silver boom nearly a century before. I was one of the latest group of would-be miners; together we were a representative cross-section of contemporary "loose" America. We were the unsettled and the dissatisfied, searching for change: change of venue, change of lifestyle, or the change that a steady paycheck might bring. We were college graduates, high school drop-outs, former cops, former crooks, laborers, white collar workers and discharged Vietnam veterans. We were eighteen years old and we were fifty; our average age was probably twenty-five.

I began my stint as a Climax miner in a series of classroom lectures explaining the mechanics of underground mining and mine safety.

As the true nature of underground mine work became apparent, so did Climax's notorious labor turnover rate; before the week long orientation was concluded, half the would-be miners had departed. Many lectures attempted to shed light on a mysterious miner's vocabulary, a bizarre language technical enough to discourage anyone looking for easy money. But safety was the predominant subject. One primary lesson stood above the others: in the underground, there are more ways to get hurt than not to get hurt.

The sheer size of the Climax mine dictated a highly-specialized system of labor diversification. A new hand would be assigned to one of a variety of work crews: Cement, Track, Mechanical or Electrical Repair, Muck, or, as was my fortune, Mine Development. I quickly learned the daily routine of the Climax miner. Each shift began with the twelve-mile drive "up the hill" to Climax. In the miners' "dry," or locker, I would change into steel-toed rubber boots, hardhat, safety eyeglasses and rubber wet suit jacket, then strap on a respirator and a heavy safety belt slinging a powder punch, pipe wrench and lamp battery. After clipping the lamp onto my hardhat, I would slip into rubber gloves and, along with 100 other miners, board the mantrip, a sheltered mine train, to rumble three-quarters of a mile into Bartlett Mountain to an interior shaft serving the lower levels.

Drift development still follows its century-old pattern, but modern tools and equipment now enable just two miners to drive a 10x12 foot haulage drift. At our heading, my partner and I were provided with compressed air and water lines, an electric trolley line, a pneumatic water pump, and a thirty-six-inch gauge railroad which we advanced along with the drift. As needed, we moved up supplies and rail-mounted equipment with an electric locomotive, or "motor." Most often, the first job on the shift would be drilling. We moved the jumbo forward to the face, then hooked up the air, water and electric lines. From the operator's platform, we controlled the movements of the twin booms and rock drills. Simultaneous operation of both drills is deafening, but ear protectors reduce it to an acceptable din. All drilling, of course, is "wet"; there is no rock dust, only a thick, eerie fog-like mist. In the large Climax haulage headings, the required 500 feet of drilling would be completed in only about an hour. Comparison of this routine performance with early drilling practices is fascinating: two double jack teams laboring continuously (if that were possible) could not manage 500 feet in twenty-four hours; four miners with a pair of smoothly-operating widowmakers (another improbability)

124

Modern underground haulage in the Climax mine. Where mining once relied on mules of the four-legged variety, Climax now utilizes "electric mules" weighing over 25 tons each and capable of pulling a twenty-car muck train loaded with 200 tons of molybdenite ore. Note the size of the miner alongside the electric locomotive.   Climax Molybdenum Company

might come close in six hours, while stacking up the same footage in dulled steels. Such comparisons are hypothetical only, for early drillers had nothing close to a ten-foot-long steel.

After drilling, my partner and I loaded the holes with 300 pounds of gelatin dynamite, timing each charge with a delay electric cap so that the first, or instantaneous, detonations would shatter the center of the rock face into a hollow, broken core. The progressive detonations would then work against that core, first collapsing the ribs, then bringing down the back, and finally raising the "lifters," the lowest row of drill holes. After connecting all the cap wires in a series circuit, we "tied in" to a live electrical blasting circuit. When miners had been posted to guard access to the shot and the traditional "Fire in the hole!" warning had been shouted, we threw the switches on the blasting box. After a ten-second series of detonations was completed, fifty tons of rock had been shattered.

125

*Modern mining at Climax. Two miners installing rock bolts and wire, a
common form of ground support and stabilization. Note the carbide lamps
have been replaced with the electric cap lamp and the drill has
become much smaller and lighter – but much more powerful and reliable –
than the early widowmakers.*

Climax Molybdenum Company

126

When the smoke and fumes had been exhausted by the mine ventilation system, we returned to the heading to bar down any loose, potentially dangerous overhead rock and bring up the pneumatic, rail-mounted mucking machine. One of us operated the machine while the other shuttled ore cars back and forth. In two or three hours, we had cleared the heading of fifty tons of muck. Then we turned to the jobs of advancing the rails and standing a new set of timber.

If everything went exactly as planned, my partner and I could "cycle" in a single shift, completing the entire development pattern to advance the drift ten feet, and leaving the following shift to repeat the performance beginning with drilling the new round. It was all clean, efficient and speedy — on paper. In the underground, it was a different story. Anything on wheels had a tendency to derail; if it were a motor or loaded ore car, getting it back on track could take hours. Even modern mine equipment fails: mucking machines beat themselves apart, car couplings break, drill steels jam in holes, and the jumbos require constant maintenance to endure the pounding of their drills. Lifter holes frequently plug under a foot of water and mud, and secondary blasting may be required. And unusually weak and dangerous ground will require additional timbering.

Modern equipment notwithstanding, all this work involves heavy physical exertion, much of it performed knee-deep in water or mud, perched precariously on the end of a timber, or in a poorly ventilated drift. Mine equipment may have changed, but human bodies are the same as they were in 1880. Fatigue comes quickly at 11,300 feet, and there is always the mental stress of trying to see the accident before it happens, whether it's falling rock, a derailing mucking machine, or a broken ladder rung.

Such conditions are normal in underground mines today, even in a mine recognized as one of the safest. Companies spend millions to comply with safety regulations and to improve working conditions, and miners work with the best of production and safety equipment. What, then, could a twelve-hour shift have been like in 1869, perhaps in the Printer Boy with hand steels, black powder and a bucket for a shaft cage? Or in the Chrysolite beside a 350-pound widowmaker? Those who have not mined will not appreciate the comparison; I myself have had to reflect on it. I found today's hardrock miner to be somewhat tougher than his counterpart in general industry, physically, of course, but even mentally in order to cope with underground conditions. If this is so today, then that 1880 hardrock miner must have been one tough son of a bitch.

Even with underground problems, most haulage headings could be cycled twice in three shifts, thus advancing the drift 500 feet in a month or more than one mile per year. Overall development proceeded rapidly, for as my partner and I worked in one heading, other crews worked simultaneously on other headings, slusher drifts, finger dashes, and even a football field-sized underground crusher room. By 1970, Climax had over thirty miles of underground railroad and a total of 150 miles of underground workings. Development and production was accompanied by the roar of drills, concussion of dynamite blasts and rumble of muck trains pervading every corner of the underground. Every day two hundred muck trains hauled 42,000 tons of ore from which, in 1970, metals worth $100,000,000 were extracted.

In terms of underground ore extraction, Climax had become one of the world's largest mines. The mill is a major industrial facility and an impressive surface sight, but the enormous underground is marked only by a portal and headframe. Through those access ways have passed enough construction materials to build a good sized town — millions of board feet of timber and incalculable tons of steel, cement and cable. Over the decades, the hollowing effect of block cave mining even reached the surface. Unable to support itself, the surface was allowed to collapse slowly into the mined-out underground, creating a half-mile-wide depression somewhat similar in appearance to a volcanic crater. This "glory hole" grew larger and more bizarre with each passing year as crumbling surface ores slowly oxidized to a garish yellow-orange. Towering far above the mill, the glory hole became the dominant feature on Fremont Pass and a symbol of Climax. Its creation, accomplished in over fifty years of continuous mining, required the underground extraction of more than a half-billion tons of ore and rock.

A century of mining, on a scale far less extensive than that at Climax, had exacted a cruel environmental toll on the highest valley of the Arkansas River. Yet those effects were small compared to the environmental problems confronting Climax, particularly in tailings disposal. For every ton of ore, Climax was left with virtually the same quantity of tailings, and what they had taken from one mountain was enough to build another. For disposal, Climax had acquired large tracts of adjacent land west of the Continental Divide on the Ten Mile drainage and eventually converted a deep, eight-mile-long mountain valley into a series of huge tailings ponds. With the passage of each ore train, a little more of Bartlett Mountain sank into the glory hole, and the spreading yellow mass that filled the ponds grew. Gradually, with both the speed and certainty of a glacier, the tailings ponds crept down from upper Ten Mile, inundating everything in their path. Buried beneath the creeping tailings were the long-abandoned town sites of Kokomo and Robinson, both bustling mining camps during the frontier booms. Of all the forgotten sites buried beneath the Climax tailings ponds, one is ironic: the site of the cabin home of old prospector Charles Senter.

The growth of the mill, the glory hole, and the tailings ponds at Climax were visually apparent; fifty years of underground change was not. Mining moved from the higher ore bodies to the lower; the original Leal and White levels were abandoned and allowed to cave into the glory hole. Later, two other main production levels, the Phillipson and the Ceresco, met a similar fate. In the 1950s, development began on a new production level, the Storke, and associated lower levels.

Climax is now employing another form of mining, an open pit which already dwarfs its previous operations. Open pitting was first attempted in the 1940s, with ore being passed to the underground for haulage. Open pitting is by far the most economical method to mine large, low grade ore bodies. But the extreme climatic conditions at Climax made the 1940 open pit impractical, for the specialized equipment that could withstand temperatures of thirty degrees below zero was not yet available. In 1878, the Breece open pit had encountered similar problems, and miners finally went underground to operate through the Leadville winter.

The Climax open pit, of course, cannot be compared with the old Breece mine. When equipment capable of alpine winter operation appeared in the 1960s, Climax began pit development with a feasibility study in 1970. An access and haulage road network was soon completed and the first open pit ore went into the crushers in 1973. New terms like slope stability and stripping ratios joined the local mining vocabulary as the pit took shape. The steepest slopes deemed stable by engineers were of country rock and stood at forty-five degrees, fractured rock from old underground workings stood at

The Climax open pit operation at Fremont Pass uses the largest and most modern equipment available to move enormous quantities of overburden and ore in the winter months at an elevation of over 12,000 feet. This drill rig, which is operated by only one man, is capable of drilling a ten-inch diameter hole forty feet deep in less than ten minutes.

Modern, high-volume haulage at the Climax open pit. Huge electric shovels with a shovel "bite" of fifteen tons are used to load diesel-electric haulage trucks that carry 170 tons of rock in a single load.

thirty-two degrees, and rock composed mostly of Paleozoic ocean sediments, laid down milleniums ago when Climax rested beneath an ancient sea, stood at thirty-seven degrees. The pit was worked in successive slices, each progressing further up the slope to gain access to the ore body.

Hardrock and open pit terminology differed, but not nearly as much as their respective equipment. Open pit drilling is performed by huge, track-mounted rigs, highly automated and operated by a single miner. A forty-foot-deep, ten-inch-diameter hole can be drilled in solid rock in less than ten minutes. A 6,500-square-foot pattern with fifty such holes is loaded with twenty-five tons — a half-ton per hole — of an ammonium nitrate-fuel oil slurry. To meet the huge explosives requirement, a contractor maintains a small, on-site plant to prepare the slurry. Detonation of a single round in the open pit produces 75,000 tons of broken rock.

131

Enormous electric shovels, receiving their power from a 6,000-volt cable and taking single-bucket bites of fifteen cubic yards (or tons), load the rock into a fleet of haulage trucks. Each of these diesel-electric trucks burns 400 gallons of fuel per day and hauls as much as 170 tons of rock in a single load. Drivers sit in a heated cabin fifteen feet above the ground and roll along on nine-foot-diameter tires.

Such high volume mining soon made it possible for the open pit miners to move 2,000,000 tons of material each month. A supporting fleet of front end loaders, bulldozers and graders worked constantly to clean rock spills and maintain the twelve-mile-long haulage road system, a demanding job considering the sub-zero temperatures, 300 inches of annual snowfall, and roads that turn to a mire in spring thaws. Every trick was used to keep the equipment rolling through the alpine winter, including use of special oils and greases, the best grades of treated diesel fuel available, heated tanks for liquids, and alcohol injection to prevent freezing in compressed air systems. The diesel equipment operated continuously for months before being shut down for servicing in cavernous mechanical service bays.

Open pit production required only forty-four miners, and in their eight-hour shift they moved 22,000 tons of rock. Recall that the Breece mine moved more ore than any other Leadville mine, 112 tons each twelve-hour shift. In 1980, Climax trucks made a total of 170 round trips in each eight-hour shift; the entire daily Breece production wouldn't even fill a single truck. Even more striking is the difference in the output of the individual miner; in 1880, a miner moved just over one ton of ore per shift, a 1980 Climax open pit miner moved 500 tons. The Leadville miner, over a period of one hundred years, had completed a remarkable transition. In 1880, he truly mined — that is, he himself tore the ore from the mountains with his hands and a few simple tools. His modern counterpart does not. Today, it is the machines that mine, tearing ore from the mountain and moving it, while the miner handles the controls. And when the inevitable accidents happen, it is now usually the machine that breaks, not the man who runs it.

The most graphic example of the changes that have come to Climax mining are seen at the deepest part of the open pit. They are gaping caverns, the exposed, abandoned workings of old underground levels. Many of today's open pit miners are the same men who drove those drifts, stood the timber, poured the cement, and laid the rail ten and twenty years ago. At that time, those drifts were the deepest, darkest

The deepest section of the Climax open pit has broken through the old sections of the underground mine. The mine foreman shown, Paul Latchaw, helped drive the drifts that his open pit crews are now breaking through. Latchaw is standing on the level of an old haulage drift. The perpendicular overhead drift is a slusher dash.

part of the underground. It now stretches the imagination to stand at what was once the underground and be able to look upward into the Colorado sky above the great open pit.

As Climax developed through the 1970s, there were also some stirrings in the old Leadville district. The district was inactive not because of ore depletion, but because of economic conditions making mining unprofitable. In 1968, the U.S. Bureau of Mines performed an extensive field survey to determine the remaining mineral resources and the future mining potential. The survey was beset with problems caused by the erratic nature in which early mining was conducted. Core drills frequently struck the rotted timbers and caved stopes of underground workings that were not even thought to exist. In their 1970 survey report, the Bureau discovered the old district to be laced with over 200 miles of underground workings, most constructed ninety years earlier.*

*TYPE OF WORKING	NUMBER	APPROXIMATE EXTENT
Shafts	1,330	80,000 feet (15 vertical miles)
Prospect Holes	1,630	16,300 feet
Tunnels	155	85,000 feet
Total Underground Workings		110,000,000 feet (over 200 miles)

About one-quarter of the shafts were open in 1949, but fewer than ten could still be examined in relative safety in 1968. Most of the old workings were caved beyond repair, their pockets of high grade ore mined out, but still containing isolated veins of very rich mineral. More significant were the large volumes of lower grade ores found throughout the district.

The Bureau of Mines estimated a total remaining district ore resource of 25,000,000 tons lying within the old workings and adjacent deposits. Included were an estimated 26,000,000 ounces of

134

silver, about ten percent of all the silver ever mined in the district. Also present are 840,000 ounces of gold in average concentrations of .04 ounces per ton, as well as significant lead and zinc values. The in situ Leadville silver and gold deposits today are worth about a quarter billion dollars each.

But don't run for a pick and shovel just yet, for the Bureau of Mines also pointed out the realities involved. District ownership, between estates, claims, fractional claims, contested claims, partnerships, leases, etc., is a very complex legal matter. If that could be resolved, profitable mining on a large scale would be possible only through a high volume approach — such as open pitting — on a vast consolidated tract. Small scale development was discouraged; contemplation of development was suggested only for technologically and financially capable corporations. The future of mining in the old district, if there is one, rests ultimately on a favorable relationship between metal prices and labor and production costs.

The last fifteen years have brought a strengthening in metal prices, especially in gold and silver. Even zinc and lead have risen by a factor of three. Not surprisingly, there were recent stirrings in the old Leadville mining district.

Mining activity began anew with development of ASARCO's Black Cloud Shaft in 1970 after years of exploration conducted by the original ASARCO corporate personage, the American Smelting and Refining Company. Production hopes rode high in 1955 when the company sank the Irene Shaft nearly 1,800 feet, the deepest of any Leadville district mine, but declining metal prices halted development in 1957. Core drill exploration continued; when prices recovered, the Black Cloud Shaft was sunk about one mile from the old Printer Boy and in the shadow of several abandoned headframes. The new workings were tied to those of the old Irene Shaft two miles north to provide the required "second escape."

In 1979, the Black Cloud employed 155 people, half in the underground. Configuration of the workings is similar to those of many early silver mines; production is handled through a single shaft and ore extracted with a stoping technique. As in the early days, the Black Cloud miners encounter ore in veins that are often erratic and elusive. The specific mining method is determined by the characteristics of the particular ore body. Since ore grade and composition varies, an assay lab is kept busy on the surface along with the 800-ton-per-day mill. Hydraulic backfill is used; mill tailings are

The modern headframe of the ASARCO Leadville Unit (Black Cloud) Mine. This headframe serves a shaft nearly 1,700 feet deep leading to 15 miles of underground workings that produced over $20,000,000 in zinc, lead, silver, and gold in 1980. Mosquito Range in background.

136

mixed with water to form a slurry which is pumped back underground to fill the mined-out stopes. Upon drying, the slurry sets up
like concrete accomplishing two important functions: re-establishing
ground support and disposing of tailings in the most environmentally
acceptable way, right back where they came from. In its first ten
years of operations, the Black Cloud mined and milled over 1,500,000
tons of ore. A ton of "average" ore contains four percent lead, eight
percent zinc, two ounces of silver and .06 ounces of gold. In 1979, the
ASARCO Black Cloud produced metals worth $20,000,000.

The similarity between the Black Cloud and early Leadville mines
ends, however, with the general configuration of underground workings. The 1,655-foot shaft is served by a three-and-one-half-ton hoist.
Fifteen miles of workings have nine producing stopes and haulage is
provided by five-ton battery-powered locomotives. Ore is dropped
through chutes to the lowest level where it is crushed before hoisting
out. Some of that ore is visually impressive high grade consisting of
white dolomite "flowers" on massive galena crystals. Newly blasted
stopes glitter brilliantly in the light of miners' cap lamps, making one
wonder what the 1880s bonanza silver ore must have looked like by
candlelight. Apart from mining equipment, another point distinguished the Black Cloud from its frontier predecessors; in its first
decade of operation, there had not been a single fatality.

Leadville's other active mine is a primary silver mine high on the
granite cliffs of the Mosquito Range. The mine is reached by a gravel
road that passes the Black Cloud, then climbs 1,000 feet above timberline, even above the Iowa Gulch Amphitheater, one of the most
beautiful alpine basins in the Rockies.

In the late 1960s, commercial grade silver ore was discovered
within the ridge that culminates at the 14,036-foot peak of Mt.
Sherman. Day Mines, Inc., a Wallace, Idaho, based company, was
contracted for development. The first ore was mined in 1974. In 1980,
the Sherman Mine employed 110 people, seventy underground. The
mine portal is at an elevation of 12,500 feet; an access tunnel runs
east into the ridge for one mile to the main production level nearly
13,000 feet above sea level. Whether the Sherman Mine qualifies as
the highest working hardrock mine in North America apparently
depends on which workings are active in a tungsten mine in the high
Sierras near Bishop, California. Twenty miles of workings wind
through the highest part of the Mt. Sherman ridge, with drifts breaking through on the eastern slope to overlook South Park. In 1980,

production was 100,000 tons of ore which yielded about fifteen ounces of silver per ton, one percent lead, and fractional gold values. The highly erratic veins made future production uncertain, even though one and one-half million ounces of silver were produced in 1980.

In 1980, both ASARCO and Day Mines conducted mineral exploration using techniques far different from those that scarred the Leadville hills with thousands of shafts and prospect holes a century ago. Simple digging has been replaced by core drilling, magnetometry and other electrical techniques. Core drilling samples the subterranean strata with hollow diamond core drills. Magnetometers detect and measure anomalies, or disturbances, in the earth's magnetic field possibly created by the presence of mineral deposits.

The mining industry has fallen under comprehensive government regulation, something the early Leadville mine owners never had to worry about. During the frontier era, the United States had rushed headlong into a land so vast many questioned if it could even be properly settled. The mineral claim system emerged as a prime proponent of the "use it and leave it" frontier land philosophies. Staking and recording gave legal right to use the land as one saw fit; walking away allowed the claim to lapse and signified not only the end of interest, but also of responsibility. Today, the highest valley of the Arkansas River is a good example of land use, abuse, and, finally, abandonment. In the mining booms, every stream was dug apart, every hill scarred with holes and heaps; and when the gold and silver was exhausted, if indeed it was ever found, the land and streams were left "as is." Although the frontier, as an historical era, died at the turn of the century, its concepts of land use proved far more durable. It was least questioned in places like Leadville where mining was the only way of life. In the 1920s, the mountain boat ran wild, tearing out the beds of three creeks without question or controversy. Even as late as World War II, to think that another hundred holes in the Leadville hills would make any difference was absurd. Who cared whether some old timer turned over a few more yards of gravel within the raped confines of California Gulch?

It was hardly coincidental that the emergence of environmental concern and compliance coincided closely with the demise of the old Leadville district in the 1950s. Leadville suddenly found itself in the unenviable position of having hundreds of old mines and no mine owners to take care of them. Higher incomes and increased mobility

138

brought more people to the Colorado Rockies and towns like Aspen — the Aspen of today, not 1885 — came into being. Their sympathies most often supported not mining, but environmentalism. Through organized and effective lobbying, they encouraged passage of environmental regulation on many levels of government to ban, discourage or otherwise restrict mining. Western mining, with its highly visible and indefensible position, became the favorite whipping boy of the conservationists. No love was lost between the opposing camps of conservation and mining. Bumper stickers supported conservationist views: "Ban Mining — Save Our Forests And Water." Mining interests retaliated: "Ban Mining — Let The Bastards Freeze In The Dark."

One look at the old Leadville district is enough to convince anyone that environmental regulation of mining is necessary. And modern mining *is* regulated, more closely than many realize. ASARCO's Black Cloud, for example, even with hydraulic backfill, must maintain a surface tailings pond. If and when mining is completed at the Black Cloud, the pond will be reclaimed and restored to include re-establishment of original contours and seeding with native grasses. When the natural vegetative growth cycles have taken over, the current residents of Iowa Gulch, about one hundred beavers, will move back in and rework the restored tailings to their own engineering specifications.

The Climax Molybdenum Company, which had already redesigned much of Fremont Pass and the Ten Mile drainage, came under similar regulation, however on a scale commensurate with that of their mining. During World War II and the Korean Conflict, the federal government had ordered Climax to maximum production for the war effort, concerned only with more molybdenum and never with tailings disposal, a problem that is now borne solely by the company. Climax has already spent millions preparing for future restoration. Many millions more will be spent, for, when mining is completed at Fremont Pass, the glory hole, the ponds and the open pit must be restored to approximate adjacent contours and replanted with native vegetation.

While complete restoration is a job for the future, significant work has already been done to safeguard water quality. Considering the size of Climax, it is remarkable that the Arkansas headwaters flow as clean as ever. All affected water is directed to the Ten Mile drainage where purification plants treat all water released below the tailings ponds. The quality of released water is far higher than that of the natural drainage, long polluted by frontier mining. Success of the Climax water program was demonstrated in 1979 when trout were stocked in Ten Mile Creek, the first time in recent memory that trout thrived in the rushing mountain river.

Tailings ponds are modern mining's most visible eyesore and draw the greatest criticism from conservationists, even demands that they be restored *now*. The ASARCO and Sherman Mine tailings draw little attention hidden in Iowa Gulch amid numerous early mine ruins and waste rock piles. The Climax ponds draw more attention along a major highway where they contrast unfavorably with the otherwise pristine beauty of the timberline country. Unfortunately, these ponds cannot be reclaimed and restored until mining is completed and the last of the mill tailings have been deposited.

Environmental compliance substantially increases mine production costs and has a major bearing on the future of mining in the United States. Unfortunately, concepts of environmental preservation and protection and financial requirements of business and availability of minerals seem to be opposing interests. But a realistic compromise must be reached. Land is no longer expendable as it once was, and minerals are more vital than ever, both strategically and to our standard of living. Policies regarding mineral development must be based on today's regulated mining industry. It must be remembered that the old Leadville district is not reflective of modern mining, nor was it solely the creation of miners and mine owners, but rather an enduring product of the American frontier land use mentality.

Regulation of modern mining also includes the areas of health and safety. Some of the most recent safety innovations stem directly from study of the 1972 Sunshine Mine (Idaho) disaster in which ninety-three hardrock miners suffocated to death in an underground fire. One was the Self-Rescuer, now mandatory equipment for anyone entering the underground. This belt-worn cannister contains a SCUBA-like mouthpiece for emergency breathing in an underground fire. Toxic carbon monoxide is absorbed and the device provides up to one hour for the miner to escape.

While working at an Arizona copper mine in 1973, I gained first-hand experience in the value of the new safety inventions, especially of the Self-Rescuer. After a freak cave-in, a fire filled the under-

140

ground with dense smoke and a toxic level of carbon monoxide. There were two fatalities, but 109 miners, including myself, were able to use the extra time provided by the Self-Rescuers to reach the surface safely. The Self-Rescuers had been issued only five days before the accident. Without them, there could have been a catastrophe and I wouldn't be here today to tell the story.

Safety regulation has greatly benefited the working miner. Most companies, however, and even some individual miners, complain that recent health and safety regulation may be somewhat overzealous and may have little to do with accident rates. Compliance with health and safety regulations requires a major company effort which further increases mine production costs.

But even with today's high mining costs in production, labor and regulatory compliance, Leadville achieved a most impressive 1980 mine production. Three mines produced eight metals valued at $300,000,000,* over half the metal production of the entire state of Colorado.

*1980 PRODUCTION OF LEADVILLE AREA MINES

METAL	PRODUCTION	VALUE (After Recovery)
Lead	7,000 tons	$4,000,000
Zinc	9,600 tons	$5,000,000
Silver	1,750,000 ounces	$25,000,000
Gold	10,000 ounces	$5,000,000
Molybdenum (Climax)	50,000,000 lbs.	
Tungsten (Climax)	2,200,000 lbs.	
Tin (Climax)	150,000 lbs.	
Iron Pyrite (Climax)	80,000,000	
Total Climax Production		$261,000,000
Total 1980 Leadville Area Mine Production		$300,000,000

In terms of mineral production, 1980 was one of Leadville's strongest years ever, one that far exceeded even the best year of the silver boom. In 1980, Leadville's three mines employed 3,400 people. The overwhelming economic dependency on mining was reflected in payrolls and local property taxes. The 1980 Climax payroll was $63,000,000, with another $5,000,000 coming across on ASARCO and Day Mines paychecks. Climax alone paid nearly three-quarters of Lake County property and school taxes, an annual assessment of $5,500,000. And virtually every business in Leadville could indirectly attribute much of its income to the mines also. The strong mining economy of 1980 single-handedly buoyed Leadville along toward what appeared to be an assured future. Climax projected an operational life of thirty-two years at the current rate of production; ASARCO projected eight years for the Black Cloud. All projections were based on existing technology and economic conditions; most believed that technological advances and higher metal prices would extend those projections considerably.

From the days of its infancy, when it was a cruel and dangerous industry, hardrock mining had made an incredible journey. A revolution had affected its every aspect. It worked first upon operational technology, replacing every tool to make possible the efficient breaking, moving and processing of rock. It continued into the organizational and economic areas as individual miners became companies which, in turn, became corporations working not bonanza mineral, but lower grade deposits once considered commercially worthless. And mining labor, health and safety had made the greatest relative advance in all of American industry. Accident rates were minimized to levels never dreamed possible. Women, once literally banned from the mines, now work together with their male counterparts in every part of the industry, including the underground. Wages do — and should — exceed those of many other industries.

The level achieved by the mining industry today was reached by a long climb up a very difficult path, one built upon tiny half-ton ore cars, giant powder, widowmaker drills, financially ruined companies and rocked up miners. Because that journey was so difficult and often tragic, the accomplishments of today are more remarkable than ever.

Mining has made great progress, but it has never been able to escape an unpredictable and often cruel economic yoke. Industry history is dominated by cycles of boom and bust dictated by the complex interaction of politics, market demand and metal prices.

142

Leadville, with near total economic dependence upon the mines, has ridden the same roller coaster, always one short step behind the rise — or fall — of mining. The discovery of gold in 1860 brought a boom to Oro City, depletion of the gravels brought a bust. Silver boomed in 1878, only to bust in 1893. World War I created another boom in 1916, the glutted metal markets of 1920 brought another bust and a long depression that didn't end until the World War II boom. By that time, Climax had become the dominant economic factor and carried Leadville through the demise of the old mining district in the 1950s. The 1970s was a strong decade; the mines and Leadville rode a solid molybdenum market and soaring free market gold and silver prices to their peak in 1980. In many respects, 1980 may have been Leadville's best year ever.

The economic unpredictability of mining was about to be demonstrated again, for, even at the peak of the 1980 boom, the harbingers of yet another bust were appearing. Gold and silver prices had reached their all-time record highs in January, 1980, and mining projections were made accordingly. But within three months, prices had plummeted; gold fell from $875 per ounce to less than $500, silver from $48 to $10. The optimistic mining projections were shattered. Even more worrisome was an imminent domestic and international business recession. The automotive and steel industries were already faltering.

The first Leadville mine to fall victim to the declining precious metal prices and a weakening national economy was the Sherman Mine, which had just passed from the control of Day Mines, Inc. to the Hecla Mining Company. In 1981, that primary silver mine was closed and 110 workers laid off. A few months later, ASARCO was forced to cut back production and employment at the Black Cloud.

But the big shock to Leadville was still coming. The economic recession worsened through 1981; by year's end, the steel industry had fallen to only 40 percent of capacity. Prices and demand for molybdenum fell. Atop Fremont Pass, the stockpiles of molybdenum grew. Climax maintained production as long as it dared. In January, 1982, more than 600 miners and millhands were laid off — the first production layoffs in over a half-century of mining. There were no improvements forthcoming in the economy or in the molybdenum market and, in June, 1982, hundreds more were laid off and production was suspended for five weeks. Another major layoff was ordered four months later and production was again suspended — this time indefinitely.

In eight months, the Leadville area mine employment had fallen from 3,400 to only 400. Without the traditional economic base, Leadville skidded into one of the nation's most severe economic depressions. The national media, which had given Leadville little attention since the silver boom, returned at last. On television and in magazines and newspapers, the name of Leadville became synonymous with unemployment and economic disaster. In July, 1982, *Newsweek* reported Leadville's economic woes in a gloomy article cleverly entitled "Rocky Mountain Low." *The New York Times* headed a similar article "Mine Town Tries to Cope;" a feature in *The Denver Post's Empire Magazine* was entitled "Hard Times Ahead." When it became clear that Climax was not about to resume production in the foreseeable future, the reaction was inevitable: suitcases were dragged out of dusty closets and "For Sale" signs went up on front lawns. By spring, 1983, Leadville's population had been cut nearly in half.

Leadville had survived many past busts, but this one would have unprecedented economic and social effects. Initially, hopes were high that the setbacks at Climax were temporary, and that production and employment would soon return to the boom levels of 1980. But Climax no longer enjoyed its historical dominance of the world molybdenum market; instead, it faced decreasing demand and growing competition from both domestic and foreign mines. Hopes slowly faded into harsh reality and, for the first time ever, Leadville realized the need to develop alternative economic bases. But, while Leadville had much potential, it also had many unique problems, the biggest of which was an unpreparedness and unwillingness to be thrust into the present.

Well over a century had passed since gold had been discovered in the highest valley of the Arkansas River. During that time, the mining industry that developed there and the city that was built to serve it had been inseparable. But now, with its mining economy finally failing, Leadville became an oddity among Colorado's mountain cities. During the 1960s and 1970s, other mountain communities eagerly sought new directions, many embracing tourism. But, just as the mountains had isolated Leadville geographically, the long-term self-sufficiency provided by mining had insulated it from change. Leadville had no need to copy contemporary standards, no reason to make itself into a facsimile of a Bavarian village. Content with its rough roads, bleached timbers and frontier ethics, Leadville had

144

never hosted rock and bluegrass festivals, think tanks or flower children. Leadville's interests were clearly reflected in its traditional "Boom Days" summer celebration, a festival of mine drilling contests and grueling burro races, events as rugged as the town itself. In civic spirit, Leadville was simultaneously tough and friendly, a curious mixture of frontier qualities long outdated in other places.

Leadville was not progressive, nor was it adulterated by the fads and trends that had homogenized much of the nation. Its proud but weathered Victorian architecture remained functional in both appearance and purpose, and was never altered for visitor's approval. Although Leadville welcomed visitors, it never sought them. There were never slick, quarter-page ads in the travel magazines, nor any "Visit Leadville" billboards cluttering the highways. When its mining economy collapsed, Leadville was an anachronism, thrust suddenly into the present and left to find its future.

Given Leadville's spectacular mountain and rich frontier history, tourism seemed to be the most obvious and immediate economic alternative. The Rockies were already a favorite place for millions of tourists to seek those elusive, remaining traces of the "real" West. But development of tourism on a scale that could replace mining was not to be a simple matter. While Leadville was indeed one of the last authentic remnants of the frontier, ironically, it was a bit too authentic. It was not in keeping with the popular image of the frontier, as represented by the made-over Dodge Cities and Deadwoods, the $10-a-ticket "Wild West" parks, or the sanitized studios of television westerns. Leadville was too real, too tough and too honest to become a major tourist attraction overnight. Leadville quickly learned that it was still a mining town, but one with little of its mining industry left to support it.

The signs of mining can be seen everywhere. Approaching Leadville from the south, one enters the highest valley of the Arkansas amid the piles of dredge tailings that mark the 65-year-old wake of the mountain boat. Nearer to Leadville, the indelible signs of mining are even more apparent. Stringtown, the southernmost part of Leadville's community sprawl, is a tiny collection of houses and mobile homes surrounded by unpainted shacks and leaning garages, all set among ridges of black slag and the tombstone-like foundations of long-gone smelters. Some slag heaps are disappearing, being hauled away for use as railroad ballast; others have been bulldozed into pseudo-functional contours to contain the mine-polluted drainage of

145

Leadville, Colorado, 1980. The mining heritage is still very much alive, as shown by this drilling contest. Mining has come a long way from hand steels; the winning miner will put two four-foot deep holes in the block of granite in three minutes.

California Gulch, a vile, rust-colored effluent in a barren gully littered with twisted pipes, corroded steam boilers and old rubber miner's boots. The mouth of the gulch is an obscene orange scar, and the original stream bed lies buried forever beneath 50 feet of lifeless, acidic mill tailings. To the east rise Carbonate, Fryer and Iron Hills, each, like a Calvary, bearing the crosses of twisted headframes, some still stubbornly standing, others rotting away on stained slopes of oxidizing waste dumps and stubbled meadows of decaying pine stumps. A large wooden sign at the beginning of Harrison Avenue tells visitors that Leadville is a National Historic District and relates some high points of its glorious history. Behind the sign, at the beginning of the business district, is a towering heap of black smelter slag—one of the inglorious legacies of that history.

146

But the glittering silver memories are here, too. Some survive in the Tabor Opera House, a sad, barn-like building, half-restored, with empty bay windows staring mournfully across the avenue at the 1879 Silver Dollar Saloon, where drinks are still served across the original bar. Alongside the opera house, in a contrast of the centuries, is a brightly lit convenience store where gaudy plastic signs advertise three-two beer and state lottery tickets. Along Harrison Avenue is a procession of weary, weathered buildings, their construction dates memorialized forever in granite blocks set among elaborate, but faded, Victorian facades. Gold pans slowly rust and gather dust in the window of a now-closed, century-old hardware store. A hand-painted sign tells visitors not to miss the old Tabor Residence only a block away; another points the way to Tabor's Matchless Mine. The Lake County Courthouse, an example of the then-avant-garde style of the 1950s, seems misplaced, unlike the office of the Leadville *Herald-Democrat*, which has a frontier look authentic enough to pass for a movie prop. Dominating Harrison Avenue is the 1885 Vendome Hotel, the original Tabor Grand Hotel, three stories of red brick standing in tired dignity, vacant, with pigeons fluttering through cracked windows in the Victorian gables. Side streets are lined with 90-year-old houses with delicate wooden latticework and peaked gables, some decrepit, others brightly restored. Between them are dozens of old shacks and garages, crooked, wandering fences and 40-year-old cars rusting slowly away on crumbling blocks.

Even as late as 1974, the Vendome was the noisy, bustling home for many transient miners; shift changes brought the heavy thump of boots on the worn staircases once climbed not only by thousands of miners, but by a United States president, a Civil War general and all of the Leadville silver barons. In the rooms, ten-foot-high ceilings loomed over brass four-posters, and original brass gas fixtures still protrude from the faded wallpaper. There was warmth and life in the old hotel then, familiar faces in the restaurant, always someone buying drinks in the bar and, inevitably, a brief fight on Saturday night. And, only a few years before that, miners could still walk to the Pioneer Bar, another of Leadville's frontier-era saloons, and purchase some commercial female companionship to go with their drinks, just as their predecessors did in the 1880s.

In the 1880s, of course, Leadville did not stand alone. It shared an economic dependency upon the mines with a host of other, lesser camps, that included Georgetown, Central City, Aspen and Breckenridge. In those camps, however, mining died decades ago. With their traditional economic base gone and their survival in question, they turned toward renewal and restoration. With an eye on the growing tourism market, they sandblasted and painted, rebuilt, tore down the old shacks and, as best they could, covered over the reminders of early mining. With imagination and creativity, they transformed themselves into centers of tourism, entertainment, recreation and the arts. The price to gain economic revitalization through blatantly commercial tourism was wholesale sacrifice of their traditional qualities and frontier character.

Had it not been for the prodigious mineralization in the old Leadville district and at Climax, Leadville would have joined the ranks of the commercial tourist towns decades ago. From time to time, community leaders had recognized the wisdom of developing a secondary economic base, one independent of mining. Incentive for action, however, always waned as the mines handed out their paychecks. Leadville never underwent contemporay nor historical restoration; instead, it underwent a natural historical *preservation* that testifies to an unwritten law regarding Colorado mining towns: that the last mine must die before a city may be truly reborn.

With its mining history and heritage as both an asset and a burden, Leadville took its first tentative steps toward an uncertain future. In March, 1983, with the governor of Colorado in attendance, Leadville embarked upon "Operation Bootstrap," a plan leading, hopefully, toward economic revitalization with the emphasis on tourism. Leadville learned that the transition from a mining economy would be neither easy nor quick. The economic revitalization plan, already in its fifth year, cannot be considered a success yet, for no alternative economies have yet been developed to replace mining. In reality, Leadville has learned to survive on a lesser economic level. Still, Leadville has undergone more change and renewal in the last five years than it had in the last century. Harrison Avenue has received a major facelift with new curbs, sidewalks, and gaslight-style street lamps. The 1886 Delaware Hotel has been completely restored and decorated in its original Victorian style. Many Victorian homes have been restored, and Leadville now hosts a very successful Christmas Victorian Homes Tour, an annual event that draws hundreds of visitors. The railroad line between Leadville and Climax, the highest line on the continent which has been inactive since 1983, is about to be reopened as a tourist attraction. Leadville also hosts the Leadville Trail 100, a 100-mile-long endurance race that annually draws some of the world's best long distance runners and national television coverage. The new event that may best reflect Leadville's new outgoing interests is an annual, month-long, summer jazz festival staged in conjunction with Loyola University of New Orleans.

Tourism, in both numbers and economic impact, continues to grow steadily, thanks also to other events that capitalize on Leadville's mining history. In 1984, a new festival, presented by Leadville's Timberline Campus of Colorado Mountain College and the people of Leadville, emerged to celebrate not the familiar silver boom years, but a forgotten aspect of local history—old Oro City. With historical authenticity a prime concern, the site of the annual Oro City festival, appropriately, is in California Gulch, not far from the site of the original gold camp of the 1860s. Over 5,000 visitors annually now enjoy superb entertainment and demonstrations of arts and crafts representative of the 1860s era. Many of the most popular exhibits are mining related, and include gold panning and placer mining, hand steel drilling, and a mine tunnel with candlelight and square-set timbering that offers an idea of what hardrock mining was like around California Gulch in the late 1860s.

The mining spirit is also evident in the annual August "Boom Days" celebration, a long weekend of events that features mine drilling contests, an unusual opportunity for non-mining visitors to observe expert miners demonstrate their skills for big cash prizes. For two days, crowds of over 1,000 people are attracted to the thunder of drills and the ring of hammers on steel. Champion hand steelers may drill through eight inches of solid granite in only five minutes, while competing miners on mechanical rock drills will go through six feet of granite in only three minutes.

Change has also come to Leadville in other ways. In 1982, California Gulch was added to the Environmental Protection Agency's National Priorities List in accordance with Superfund legislation. Unlike many industrial Superfund sites, the sources of pollution here are both numerous and complex. The earliest man-made pollution sources may be traced back to the placer mining of the 1860s. Today, literally thousands of inactive or abandoned shafts, tunnels, waste heaps, ditches and prospect holes, controlled by hundreds of different owners, all contribute in varying degrees to the acidic, heavy metal pollution that plagues California Gulch and, subsequently, the Arkansas River. The long process of Environmental Protection Agency field investigation and feasibility studies has progressed slowly. Although questions of responsibility and liability remain, clean-up action may soon begin.

While Leadville's interests have expanded beyond the traditional mining parameters, mining itself, although depressed, is not dead. Even though a severe general depression in western metal mining has restructured and trimmed down the entire industry, the ASARCO Leadville Unit—the Black Cloud Mine—has remained an important producer of lead, zinc, silver and gold. The 140 jobs it provides for the Leadville area have never been more appreciated.

Thanks to the high prices of gold, gold mining has been greatly stimulated in the West and increased activity is even seen in the old Leadville mining district. Three small, highly selective hardrock mines are now under development and should begin production soon, providing thirty mining jobs. Interestingly, one of those new mines is located on Printer Boy Hill at the head of California Gulch. New drifts have broken into the 120-year-old workings of the original Printer Boy, revealing wooden ladders and timbers from Leadville's first hardrock mine in a remarkable state of preservation. A reminder of just how dangerous hardrock mining can be occurred in September, 1987, and put Leadville in the national news. Five miners at one of the developing gold mines were trapped 600 feet below the surface following an accident in the shaft. Fortunately, there were no deaths or injuries; after 28 hours of entrapment, the five miners were rescued.

Leadville also hosts another mineral recovery operation that represents a relatively new aspect of western metal mining with considerable potential—reprocessing of old mine wastes. At a small mill at the south end of Harrison Avenue, a dozen employees are reprocessing old mill tailings from California Gulch. Using a flotation separation process, pyrite—iron sulfide—is recovered and sold for use as a coloring agent in glass manufacture.

The current mining activity is almost lost in the old Leadville mining district, 20 square miles of old headframes, ore chutes, access roads, tramways and mine dumps that are one of the West's greatest graveyards of frontier mining. In both number and concentration, the ruins reflect the intensity of mining during the silver era and the wartime metal booms. Visitors' impressions of the ruins vary greatly with their individual sense of history; they may be viewed either as a

Weathered headframes, twisted cables, rusted ore buckets . . . all tell the real history of Leadville, Colorado.

151

colossal junk pile or a superb, however unpolished, arena of history.

The road into California Gulch passes the site where Abe Lee and his partners struck gold, writing the first chapter of what would become Leadville's grand mining epic. The gulch is now lined with the reminders of yesterday's mining: the 1895 Resurrection Mill that disgorged most of the tailings that now bury the gulch; the Yak Tunnel, now a major pollution source, still faithfully draining scores of abandoned mines; the 1907 substation that brought the first electrical power to the mines; and the site of old Oro City with its rotting cabins, nameless headframes, and the nearly vanished ruins of the old Printer Boy Mine, where men used hand steels and black powder to mine extraordinary specimens of crystalline gold on white quartz.*

Ore has long rolled along this road, first in wagons, most recently in heavy trucks hauling the lead-silver and zinc-gold concentrates from the Black Cloud Mine. The road winds beneath forgotten headframes, now lonely sentries guarding crumbling shafts and the memories of the men who worked them. A few old mines still cling to their original names—Silent Friend, Maid o'Erin, Little Ellen, Fanny Rawlings, Clear Grit—names that invoke an oddly personal quality to their lifeless ruins and hint at immortality, at further riches still waiting to be mined.

Scattered among the mines lie frayed cables, rusted ore buckets, twisted rail and half-buried ore cars that once conveyed the glittering ores from the tunnel-ridden hills. Even a casual search will turn up the chipped, rusted hand steels that once led the way through the hard rock, their cutting edges long dulled, their tops mushroomed by hammer and muscle. An eerie silence prevails as the mountain wind whispers an eloquent soliloquy to yesterday's miners who, it seems, were suddenly and inexplicably called away from their work, leaving behind their tools and dreams for someone yet to come.

Leadville's mining heritage and history is the most comprehensive and continuous in the United States. Every form of metal mining ever conducted in the American West was employed here at one time or another. The mining epic that began 128 years ago with nothing but shovels and gold pans would eventually include sluicing, hydraulicking, mechanical and suction dredging, draglining, a remarkable open

---

*Six such specimens, part of the Frank C. Allison Collection, are on permanent display at the Arthur Lakes Library, Colorado School of Mines, Golden, Colorado. These specimens are from the Leadville District, probably from the Printer Boy in upper California Gulch.

152

From high above the old mining district, a solitary headframe from the 1880s looks down over the city of Leadville and west toward the Continental Divide.

pit operation, and every conceivable approach to hardrock mining. All those methods, together with the efforts of tens of thousands of Leadville miners, made possible an overall Leadville area metal production of over two billion dollars. Considering the geography and climate, the difficulties of early mining and the relatively small area from which the metals were taken, there are few mining districts in the world that can hold the proverbial miner's candle to Leadville.

Recognition of that rich mining heritage finally came in December, 1986, when Leadville was chosen to become the site of the National Mining Hall of Fame and Museum. The federally chartered institution will be more than a museum, but a library, research facility and conference center, and will eventually be developed into a showcase for the American mining industry. When the museum opens in 1988, it will present a comprehensive picture of American mining from

153

Indian times to the present. Exhibits will cover mining methods, mining transportation, geology, mineral uses, assaying and prospecting. There will also be an extensive mineral and ore collection, as well as a Hall of Fame honoring individuals who have influenced the course of American mining.

Yet another event has recognized Leadville's mining past and perhaps future. In November, 1987, Leadville hosted the first annual Colorado Mining Summit, a public forum involving the mining industry, state and federal regulatory agencies, and environmental interests. Attended by Colorado's governor and over 400 others, the Mining Summit offered an exchange of information and viewpoints that will hopefully re-establish an economic and regulatory balance, allowing mining to regain strength.

Leadville's grand mining epic has not yet run its course. The gold, the silver and the molybdenum have written spectacular chapters in Leadville's history, but mining has compromised the natural beauty of the land about which Pike and Frémont wrote so eloquently. Mining has scarred the land, polluted the water and air, leveled forests and killed the game. Mining the billions of dollars of metal also had a human cost, paid for with the hundreds of lives lost in the dark drifts beneath the earth.

Miraculously, the land has proven both resilient and forgiving; there are some scars that will never heal, but the air is clean again and herds of game roam the deep mountain forests. Final payment for the reckless glories of frontier mining will be made when water quality is restored. Mining, as the economic journals report, is "depressed." But the industry is also undergoing a major economic and technical transition. And, as Leadville moves toward a new, diversified economy, mining will return to play a new, and still important, role.

SOURCE ESSAY

This account of the Leadville story has been written not from the standpoint of a scholar or historian, but rather from that of a working miner. Accordingly, I have adopted an informal style which a miner might use in recounting a tale, and have dispensed with the footnotes and detailed source documentation that might accompany a textbook or formal reference work.

My impressions of modern mining come directly from my own experience as a hardrock miner with the Climax Molybdenum Company, Climax, Colorado, and in the copper mines of Arizona and the uranium mines of Wyoming. Many of these underground shifts were spent in conversation with men of twenty or thirty years seniority who, in their youth, had hand mucked from iron sheets and drilled "off the column." They, in turn, had learned their mining from men who had drilled with widowmakers by the beam of a carbide lamp and who even recalled the final end of the hand steel era in the 1920s. I gathered other ideas on early mining from Mr. Alexander McLaughlin and Mr. Pablo Donato Rego who, in the mountains of the Republic of Honduras, permitted me the honor of working briefly in their lead-silver mine with methods only a short step above those of the 1880s. My impressions of placer mining, particularly that gold does not lie about on top of the gravels "winking" at one, come from a long season of sluicing in the Alaskan bush.

The technical and historical data, to the best of my knowledge, is accurate. My sources include the early Leadville newspapers, Lake County (Colorado) Courthouse records, annual reports and other publications of the Colorado Bureau of Mines (now the Colorado Division of Mines), publications of the United States Bureau of Mines, and company publications of ASARCO, Inc., the Climax Molybdenum Company, Day Mines, Inc., E. I. DuPont de Nemours Company, the Ingersoll-Rand Company, and the New York Engineering Company. A particularly informative source was *A Treatise on Explosive Compounds, Machine Rock Drills, and Blasting*, by Henry S. Drinker (Colorado School of Mines).

General historical background of Leadville and early Colorado mining was provided by many books including: Duane Smith's *Colorado Mining* and *Rocky Mountain Mining Camps: The Urban Frontier*; Frank Hall's *History of the State of Colorado*; Ed Blair's *Leadville: Colorado's Magic City*; Charles Henderson's *Mining in Colorado; A History of Discovery, Development, and Production*; O. L. Baskin's *History of the Arkansas Valley, Colorado*; Otis Archie King's *Gray Gold*; Otis Young's *Western Mining*; Martin Lingfelter's *Hardrock Miners*; Mark Wyman's *Hardrock Epic*; and Robert Wallace's *The Miners*. I also drew upon my own articles in *The Denver Post's Empire Magazine* and my first book, *The Making of a Hardrock Miner*.

I would also like to thank the following who, in their own areas, provided great assistance: Mr. Pat Wadsworth, Public Relations Manager, and Mr. Paul Latchaw, Open Pit Shift Foreman, Climax Molybdenum Company, Climax, Colorado; Mr. Gordon Kidd, Manager — Employee Communications, ASARCO, Inc., New York, New York; Mr. Dave Lewis, Unit Manager, and Mr. Terry Tew, Mining Engineer, ASARCO Leadville Unit (Black Cloud), Leadville, Colorado; Mr. Ralph Noyes, Superintendent, Day Mines' Sherman Mine, Leadville, Colorado; Mr. Dave Parry, Curator of the Colorado Mountain History Collection and Director of the Lake County Public Library, Leadville, Colorado; Dr. John Shannon, Professor of Geology and Museum Director, Colorado School of Mines, Golden, Colorado; and the staffs of the Denver Public Library Western History Collection and the Library of the Colorado Historical Association, both in Denver, Colorado, and the Arthur Lakes Library of the Colorado School of Mines, Golden, Colorado.

GLOSSARY

Alloy. A combination of two or more elemental metals producing a single metal with desirable or improved chemical or physical properties.

Amalgamation. A gold recovery process in which mercury is used to dissolve finely divided bits of gold in placer concentrates or crushed ores.

Assay. A test to determine the metal content of a mineral or ore. Precious metal assays are conventionally expressed in Troy ounces per ton; base metal assays are expressed in percent by weight.

Backfill. Waste rock or tailings used to fill a stope after removal of ore; hydraulic backfill is waste rock or tailings pumped back underground as a water slurry.

Base Metals. Any one of the common metals such as lead, copper, zinc, etc.

Cage. The moveable structure within a mine shaft that is fixed to the hoist cable and used for vertical conveyance of men and material.

Cageway. The section in a shaft through which the cage moves. Also, the channel structure within a shaft which guides the movement of the cage.

Collar. The mouth of a shaft or the uppermost frame of a shaft. Also, the beginning of a drill hole; the point at which the drill steel first penerates the rock.

Color. Tiny particles of metallic gold found in a gold pan.

Consumption. A general frontier term referring to the debilitating effects of all pulmonary disorders.

Core Drill. A drill that removes a cylindrical section of the rock formation penetrated for purposes of examination.

Dragline. A continuous, moveable cable mounting buckets or scrapers used to move surface gravels in placer mining.

Dredge. Any mechanical or hydraulic device used to move submerged placer gravels to sluices.

Drift. A horizontal underground passage.

Face. The vertical section of rock exposed by blasting; the end of a drift or tunnel to be advanced.

Float. Fragments of a mineral that have become separated from an outcrop or lode deposit.

Flour Gold. In placer mining, the finest particles of gold that are sometimes lost with the tailings.

Flux. Any chemical, metal or rock added to a smelter charge to combine with and remove undesirable materials and impurities.

Grubstake. Financial backing for a mining or prospecting venture in return for a share of the mine's value, if any.

Hardrock Mining. Mining in which drilling and blasting must be employed to break rock. Also, a general term for underground metal mining.

Headframe. The steel or timber frame over a shaft mounting the sheave wheel.

Highgrading. the practice of stealing especially valuable pieces of ore.

Hoist Shack. The structure to the rear of the headframe housing the hoist winch and power source.

Hydraulicking. The use of powerful water pumps to erode away alluvial gravels in placer mining.

Lode Deposit. Quartz or other rock in place bearing a valuable mineral deposit.

Mineral. Any chemical element or compound occurring naturally as a result of inorganic processes. Minerals are the constituents of rocks. Also, the general frontier term for ore.

Muck. Rock or ore broken by blasting.

Nipper. A miner assigned to move material and tools within a mine.

Open Pit. A mine with workings open to the surface.

Ore. A metal-bearing mineral, or mineral aggregate, that is profitable to mine.

Outcrop. A mineral lode deposit at or very near the surface.

Overburden. The layer of barren, worthless material that must be removed to expose valuable minerals in open pit or placer mining.

Panning. Use of a gold pan to separate placer gold from gravels. The simplest form of placer mining.

Placer Deposit. An alluvial concentration, usually formed by river action, containing gold or other valuable minerals or metals.

Placer Mining. The extraction of gold, or other valuable minerals or metals, from alluvial deposits by washing with water.

Portal. The surface opening of a horizontal, inclined or declined tunnel.

Refractory Ores. Ores, usually complex, that require special or difficult smelting processes.

Shaft. A vertical mine opening giving access to underground workings.

Sheave Wheel. The pulley wheel mounted atop the headframe that conveys the hoist rope or cable into the shaft.

Slag. Smelter waste.

Sluice. A long wooden or metal trough with riffles fixed to the bottom; used for recovering gold from placer gravels.

Smelting. The reduction of metal ores or ore concentrates in furnaces to produce molten metal and molten slag.

Stamp Mill. A frontier-era mechanical device used to crush ores.

Stope. An underground working from which ore has been extracted.

Tailings. The waste portion of ore or gravels after extraction of the valuable minerals.

Timbering. The wooden supports and braces used to stabilize underground workings.

Tramping. The tendency among miners of frequently moving from job to job; the basis of the high labor turnover that has traditionally affected the mining industry.

Waste Rock. The barren rock removed from a mine to allow access to ore.

Whim. A large capstan with one or more radiating arms to which a horse or horses may be yoked. Used for hoisting.

Widowmakers. The early "dry" mechanical rock drills which were the cause of widespread silicosis among miners.

Windlass. A simple hoisting device, often manually powered, used in small mines on which the hoist rope is wound around a horizontal drum.

Winze. A vertical passage connecting interior levels in a mine.

INDEX

Alma, 28
American Metals Company, 97, 100, 102
Aspen, 48, 80-81, 139, 148

Bartlett Mountain, 62-63, 87, *98*, 99, 105, 110, 116, *120*, 121, 139, 149
Black Hills gold rush, 28
black powder, 22-23, 32-33
blasting, 22-23, 53-57, 101, 108, 125, 131
"Boom Days" celebration, 152
Box Creek, 109
Breckenridge, 11, 148
Breece Hill, 73
Brooks, John W., 33
Burleigh, Charles, 33-34
Burleigh mechanical drill, 34-36, 79
Busk-Ivanhoe Tunnel, 80

California, 9, 11
California Gulch, 11, 13, 16-24, 28-29, 62, 75, 83, *85*, 138, 146-147, 149
Canterbury Tunnel, 105
carbide lamp, 90, 92, *111*, 117
Carbonate Hill, 29, 37, 73, 84, 147
Caribou, 27

Central City, 9, 18, 148
Climax Molybdenum Company, 97, *98*, 100-102, 104-105, 109-110, *111*, 112-116, 119, *120*, 121, 123-*125*, 128-129, 131, 134, 139-144, 149
Climax, town of and railroad stop, 87, 96-97, 102-105, 112, 116-117, *120*
Colorado Gulch, .11
Colorado Militia, 82
Colorado Power Company, 92, 106
Colorado School of Mines, 88, 150
Colorado Springs, 29
Colorado & Southern Railroad, 114
company towns, 104, 116-117, *120*
contract mining, 69-71
contributory negligence, 59
copper, 82, 89, 99, 110, 115, 121, 144
Cornish influence on mining, 22, 33, 48, 61, *68*-69
Couch, J., 33
Cripple Creek, 81, 148
Currier, John, 11

Day Mines, Inc., 137, 141, 143

Deadwood (South Dakota), 41
Denver, 6, 9, 13, 17, 24-25, 31,
    36, 62, 83, 90, 92, 97
Denver Post Empire Magazine,
    144
Denver & Rio Grande Railroad,
    80
Denver & South Park Railroad,
    87
Derry Dredge, 106-*107*, 108-109
dynamite, 22, 32-33, 50, 52, 90

electricity, introduction of, 90,
    92-93, 101, 117

Fairplay, 6-7, 9, 20
fellow servant liability, 59
Ford Motor Company, 102
Fremont, John C., Col., 8
Fremont Pass, 62-63, 87, 99,
    105, 110, 116, *120*-121, 139,
    143
French, exploration by, 6
Fryer Hill, 29, 37, 40, 66, 73-74,
    84, 105, 147

Gates, Stephen F., 33
Georgetown, 9, 27-28, 34, 69,
    148
"giant" powder, 33, 47, 50, 52,
    73
gold, 6, 8-24, 27-28, 62, 71-72,
    75, 81-84, 89, 99-100,
    105-106, 108-110, 115-116,
    121, 135, 137-138, 141, 143,
    150, 154
Granite, 11, 20, 109

Hagerman Tunnel, 80

hand drilling, 22-23, 29, 36, 88,
    93, *94*, 124-125, 152
hand drilling contests, *94*, 143,
    146, 152
Hecla Mining Company, 143
highgrading, 71-73
Hook, George, 38-39

Idaho Springs, 9, 18
International Hydraulic
    Dredge Company, 109
Iowa Gulch, 16, 137, 139-140
iron, 75, 89, 121
Iron Hill, 29, 37, 73, 84, 105, 147
iron pyrite, 115, 141

Jurich, Lazar, 85

Kelley, A. G., 11
King, Otis Archie, 96-97, 100
Kokomo, 129
Korean Conflict, 115, 139

labor unions, 65-66, 82, 116
Lake City, 28
Lake County, 20, 25, 109
Lake Creek, 7, 106, 109
lead, 18, 29-30, 38, 67, 72, 75,
    89, 105, 110, 114-115, 121,
    135, 137-138, 141
Leadville Herald Democrat, 147
Leadville Mine Drainage
    Tunnel, 115
Leadville Weekly Herald, 13, 56,
    58, 75
leasing, 70-71, 105
Lee, Abe, 11-13, 15, 149
Leyner, J. George, 34-35, 79, 92
Leyner mechanical drill, *91*-92

Lovell, William "Chicken Bill," 39

manganese, 89, 121
mechanical rock drill, 33-36, 49-*51*, 77-80, *91*-93, 101, 108, *111*, 117, 124-*126*, *130*-131, *146*, 152
Metalgesellschaft, 97
mine
  accidents, 43-46, 48-50, 52-60, 81, 84, 92, 94-95, 103, 112, 119, 27, 140-141
  bureaus, 75-76, 94-95, 108, 110, 114-115, 117, 121, 134-135
  haulage, 46-*47*, 75, 92-93, 101-102, 132-*133*
  workings, extent of, 74-76, 128, 134, 137
Mines
  American Flag, 24
  Black Cloud Shaft (ASARCO, Inc.), 135-*136*, 137, 139-141, 143-144, 149-150
  Breece, 75, 129, 132
  Chrysolite, 39, 49, 66, 73-75, 127
  Comstock (Nevada), 21, 35, 74
  "Downtown" mines, 77, 114
  Five-Twenty, 24
  Ibex, 82, 89
  Irene Shaft, 135
  Little Chief, 49, 66
  Little Jonny, 82
  Little Pittsburg, 38-39, 73
  Matchless, 39, 147
  Pilot Tunnel, 24

  Printer Boy, 24-25, 72, 127, 135, 150
  Robert E. Lee, 40, 74
  Sherman, 137, 140, 143-144, 149, 150
  Union-Smuggler (Aspen), 48
mining
  cave block system, 101-102, 128
  environmental effects, 15, 19, 67, 83-84, 108-109, 128-129, 138-140, 146-147, 154
  hardrock, 20-24, 27-*30*, *31*, 32-41, *42*, 43-*64*, 66-*68*, 69-84, 88-*91*, 92-97, 99-105, 109-*111*, 112-*113*, 114-*118*, 119, 121, 123-*125*, *126*-128, 131, 134-*136*, 137, 143, *151*-152
  open pit, 75, 129-*130*, *131*-132, *133*, 135
  placer, 13-*14*, 15, 19, 28, 64, 106-*107*, 108-109
  draglining, 116
  dredging, 106-*107*, 108-109
  hydraulicking, 28
molybdenite, 88-89, 96, 100
molybdenum, 87-89, 96, 99-102, 109, 112, 114-116, 119, 128, 141, 143-144, 154
Mosquito Range, 3, 7, 11-12, 18, 20, 37, 59, 62, 137, 145
Mowbray, George, 32
mules, haulage, 46-*47*, 92-93, 101
Mullen, Charles, 22

New York Engineering Company, 106, 108-109

New York Times, 144
Newsweek, 144
nitroglycerin, 31-35, 50, 52, 90
Nobel, Alfred, 32

Oro City, 13, 16-18, 20-25,
    27-29, 38, 40, 73, 83, 143, 150

Panic of 1893, 81
Phillipson, Brainard, 100, 102
Pike, Zebulon, Capt., 7-8, 154
Pikes Peak gold rush, 9-*10*, 11,
    20, 27, 81
de Pratz, Le Page, 6
pulmonary problems, 59, 65,
    77-79
Purcell, James, 5-8, 144

Rafferty, Issac, 11
Resurrection Mill, 149
Rische, August, 38-39
Robinson, 129

St. Louis, 6, 29
Santa Fe, 7
Scheele, Carl, 88
Schott, Max, 97
Self-Rescuer, 140-141
Senter, Charles, 62-63, 87-88,
    96-98, 110, 129
Sherman Silver Purchase Act,
    81
silicosis, 77-79, 81
silver, 18, 21-30, 36-40, 43, 48,
    59, 67, 69, 71-77, 81-82, 84,
    89, 99, 100, 110, 114-115,
    121, 135, 137-138, 141, 143,
    150, 154
    native (horn), 75
Silver Plume, 9, 34

Silverton, 28
Singer, Issac, 33
Slabtown, 29
Slater, S. S., 11
smelters, 24, 27-29, 67, 75,
    83-*85*, 89, 99, 116
Smith, Cooper, 22
South Park, 1, 5-7, 11, 137,
    143-144, 149, 150
Spanish, exploration by, 6, 8
steam power, introduction of,
    33, 45
Stevens, George, 11
Stevens, William, 28
Stringtown, 146
Sunshine Mine disaster (Idaho),
    140

Tabor, Augusta, 18-19, 24
Tabor, Baby Doe, 67
Tabor Grand Hotel, 67, 123,
    147, 148
Tabor, Horace Austin Warner,
    18-19, 24, 38-39, 67, 123, 148
Ten Mile Creek, 62, 87, 129,
    139-140
Tennessee Pass, 80
timbering, square-set, 48
Timkin Roller Bearing
    Company, 102
tin, 115, 141
tramping, 67-69, 80, 104-105
Travelers' Insurance Company,
    60
tungsten, 115, 137, 141

Western Federation of Miners,
    82
Webster, Anthony D., 16
"widowmakers," *51*, 78-79, 93

Wood, Alvinus, 28
World War I, 96-101, 143
World War II, 114-115, 138-139, 145

Yak Tunnel, 92, 150

zinc, 82, 89, 99, 110, 114-115, 121, 135, 137, 141